QUES
BALANCE

QUEST FOR
BALANCE

The Human Element in Performance Management Systems

André A. de Waal

John Wiley & Sons, Inc.

Library of Congress Cataloging-in-Publication Data:
De Waal, André.
  Quest for balance : the human element in performance management systems / André A. de Waal.
    p. cm.
Includes bibliographical references.
  ISBN 0-471-20571-0 (cloth : alk. paper)
1. Organizational effectiveness.   2. Industrial management.   I. Title:
Human element in performance management systems.   II. Title.
  HD58 .9 .D4 2002
  658.4'02—dc21

                                                    2002000626

CONTENTS

INTRODUCTION

The importance of performance management systems for an efficient and effective management information supply in an organization has increased over the last decade. In order for organizations to be able to handle the continuous increase in information and to be successful in turbulent environments, they need an efficient performance management system, such as the balanced scorecard. At the same time, the roles of change management and managerial behavior in change processes have become more visible. Implementing a new performance management system is often a major change for an organization. It, therefore, stands to reason that human behavior and managerial style should also play a prominent role during the implementation and use of such a system. This book examines the role of the human element in the successful implementation and use of a performance management system.

As a consultant, I observed firsthand how important the role of the human element can be. In particular, during one engagement, I had a conversation with the CEO of an organization at which I helped to implement a new performance management system. We were discussing how the organization was getting along with the new system. The CEO was complaining that one manager in particular was not using the new system at all. I interrupted him and said: "Let me guess, you mean Mr. X." The CEO reacted with surprise: "You are right. How did you know?" I explained to him that I had gotten to know Mr. X during the interviews and workshops I had conducted with the management team. All those times, Mr. X, who was the creative director of the organization, had been very enthusiastic about the new performance management system—it appealed to his sense of creativity—and he had been heavily involved in the implementation. But now that the system was finalized and in operation, the novelty had worn off and he was no longer interested. In contrast, his colleague Mr. Y, the operations director, took a long time to realize the added value of the new performance management system. But as soon as the system was operational, Mr. Y turned out to be a real advocate, as it fitted his need for control. I was able to make a calculated guess because I knew both persons and had observed their behavior firsthand. After the conversation with the CEO, I thought to myself: Wouldn't it be great if you could, during the implementation of a new performance management system, predict beforehand which person would be using the system and which one would not? Then, you could tailor the project approach and tailor the new system to take these differences in managers' behaviors and styles into account. I decided to start a search for the behavioral aspects of managers that are important to a successful implementation and use of a performance management system. With the results of this investigation, I hoped to be able to discover the features of performance management systems that are better balanced than traditionally is the case. Ideally these balanced systems would be used more regularly and frequently by managers.

MANAGEMENT SUMMARY

Performance measurement and control systems are defined in the management literature as formal, information-based routines and procedures that managers use to maintain or alter patterns in organizational activities.[1] These systems focus on conveying financial and nonfinancial information that influence decision making and managerial action. The recording, analysis, and distribution of this information is embedded in the processes of the organization, and is often based on predetermined practices at preset times in the business cycle.

Performance management systems are designed specifically to be used by managers. The main reason for managers to use a performance management system is to influence the behavior of subordinates. To do so successfully, managers need a clear view of human nature and behavior. Consequently, there is a need for some sort of framework for the identification of those personality factors that are important for managerial behavior and attitudinal reactions to performance management systems. This need for more knowledge about performance management systems ties in with the idea that there is a natural evolutionary cycle at work in the development of theory and practice in the field of performance management systems: At first, organizations realized they were measuring the wrong things (late 1980s and early 1990s), after that organizations adopted and implemented new and alternative performance management systems (the 1990s), and finally organizations asked the question how to use the data provided by the new performance management system in a better way (late 1990s and the beginning of the twenty-first century).[2]

Performance can be considered an outcome of both organizational and human activities. Originally, performance measures were used as surrogates for performance outcomes, and a direct link between performance management systems, human nature, and outcomes was not made. This shortcoming was first addressed in the early 1950s, when the human behavioral side of performance management systems use was explored for the first time, looking specifically at the budgeting system.[3] It was concluded that budgets and budgeting processes could be associated with important human relation problems. These included worker–management separation, cross-boundary conflict, and job-related tension. This conclusion was a substantial departure from the mechanistic approach to performance measurement found in traditional management theory. Since then, the issue of the human element received more attention in the literature, although a lot of this attention is still focused on its relationship to the budgeting system.

In recent years, an increasing number of organizations have implemented a performance management system that is based on critical success factors (CSFs) and key performance indicators (KPIs). A frequently used format in this context is the balanced scorecard (BSC), developed by Kaplan and Norton.[4] Despite the increase in experience gained with these systems, there is still a lot to be learned about the factors that influence the everyday use of a performance management system. Most research in the field of performance management systems has been focused on the technicalities of implementing such a system, rather than on management and human behavior issues. As a consequence, the role of managerial behavior in the use of a performance management system has thus been underexposed in previous research.

Two recent studies into the behavioral aspects of performance management system implementation and performance management system use aim at filling this void. The first study found that managers' cognitive limitations, that is, the way in which managers regard their surroundings, may prevent organizations to fully benefit from a performance management system, and that cognitive differences between managers may result in different uses of the performance management system.[5] The second study found that positive outcomes from performance management system use were mostly determined by the effectiveness by which it was used as a management control device (defined in terms of effective measurement and comprehensive performance), and that these outcomes were not attributable to its use as a communication device.[6] Positive outcomes were generated when behavior of employees was aligned with strategy and when employees were motivated. This indicated the existence of causal relationships between performance management system design and control use, managerial and employee behavior, and organizational performance.

In this book, the line of research into the behavioral aspects of performance management system implementation and use is followed by investigating the question: *Which behavioral factors contribute to the successful implementation and use of a performance management system?* This question is answered by analyzing three organizations that have designed and implemented a new performance management system. The design and implementation of a new system is regarded successful when managers use the system on a day-to-day basis. The investigation aims to identify the behavioral factors that are important to this success. Many behavioral factors have been suggested in the literature. Examples are: "Managers accept the need for performance management," "Managers do not experience the new performance management system as threatening," and "Managers accept the project promoter."

My investigation used the method of case study research, which was conducted at three organizations: a nonprofit organization, a for-profit company, and an organization in transition from nonprofit to for-profit. These organizations all had, at the time of the research, extensive experience with a performance management system. Generally, in a performance management system implementation project, three stages can be distinguished. In the *starting stage,* an organization takes the decision to implement a performance management system. In the *development stage,* customized CSFs, KPIs, and a BSC are developed. In the *use stage,* an organization starts to use the performance management system. In each stage, identification of those behavioral factors that were the most important to a successful conclusion of that stage took place. In addition, the stage that was the most important to the regular use of the performance management system was identified.

The research results indicate that, contrary to my expectations, the way in which the *starting* and *development* stages were carried out, appeared to be nondecisive for the daily use of the performance management system after its implementation. The results also indicate that 18 specific behavioral factors do appear to be important for the day-to-day use of the performance management system.

It became clear during the investigation that there seemed to be a relation between the success of a performance management system (in terms of frequent daily use) and the attitude of managers toward a performance management system. As the aspects of cognitive and interpersonal abilities of managers were not explicitly taken into account so far, and because it seemed these were important to a successful performance management system, I decided to start a second investigation in which I concentrated on the correlations between performance management system use, management styles, and organizational performance.

Management styles are composed of the cognitive and interpersonal abilities of managers and become apparent in individual competencies and observable behaviors of managers. In this respect, a competence is a feature of an individual that has a causal relationship with effective and/or excellent behavior at performing a certain task or in a certain situation. Management styles are considered one of the important and permanent drivers of managerial behavior. Developers and users of performance management systems should take these management styles into account when they are developing and implementing a new system.

The second investigation focused strictly on observable behavior. My objective was to find answers to the following questions: *Which management styles are related to which types of performance management system use?* and *Do specific management styles and types of performance management system use have an effect on organizational performance?*

To this end, I formulated several assumptions about the relationships between managerial styles, types of performance management system use, and organizational performance. These assumptions were tested, using a self-constructed questionnaire, at 12 organizations that had experience with a performance management system.

The results indicate that differences in types of performance management system use can (at least partly) be explained by differences in management styles as well as by differences in type of organizations (profit versus nonprofit and manufacturing versus nonmanufacturing). The results also indicate that the use of a performance management system raises the productivity and the overall quality of an organization, that one specific management style, namely that of being flexible and adapting easily to different organizational circumstances, increases the quality of the work delivered, and finally that the management style of teamwork and cooperation increases the productivity.

The implication of my investigations are that further research in behavioral factors, types of performance management system use, types of organizations, and management styles is recommended, to strengthen the frequent, day-to-day use of a performance management system and to improve organizational results.

BOOK SETUP

The setup of this book is depicted in Exhibit I.1. In Part One of the book, the development history of performance management systems is

Exhibit I.1   Schematic Overview of the Book

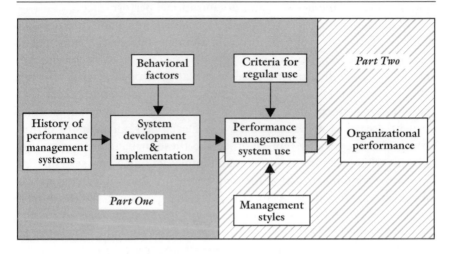

briefly discussed (Chapter 1). This is followed by a description of the behavioral factors that are important for the successful implementation and use of a performance management system as well as the so-called criteria for regular use, which denote whether the use of the performance management system is of value to the organization and its managers (Chapter 2). By means of case study research, the behavioral factors that are important for successful performance management system use are identified (Chapter 3).

In Part Two, a description is given of which management styles of a manager are important for which specific type of performance management system use, and whether specific management styles and specific types of performance management system use improve the performance of an organization (Chapters 4 and 5).

This book describes the results of an investigation into how to develop a better balanced performance management system by taking the human element into account. As such, this book has practical value to organizations. The introduction of CSFs, KPIs, and the BSC can have a far-reaching impact on an organization and its managers. Unfortunately, many organizations underestimate this impact on the motivation and attitude of managers. By taking into account beforehand possible consequences of a new performance management system on the styles and behavior of people, the implementation approach can be adapted in such a way that the introduction of a new system can be made easier. This is even more important, as a survey into best practices in the area of restructuring at 211 European companies across all industries found that

Exhibit I.2 **Types of Restructuring Obstacles, in Percentage of Survey Respondents**

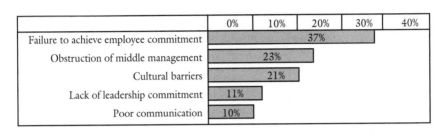

Source: Kröger, F., M. Träum, and M. Vandenbosch (1998). *Superheading growth: How Europe's top companies are restructuring to win.* London: Pitman Publishing.

the vast majority of restructuring obstacles are related to behavioral issues (Exhibit I.2). The conclusion of the survey was that "getting the people issues right" is critical because this will improve an organization's performance. However, at the same time, it was noted that many organizations still have a hard time getting the human element right.

Getting the people issues right is critical because this will improve an organization's performance. This book aims at helping organizations getting it right the first time around.

ENDNOTES

1. Simons, R. (2000). *Performance measurement and control systems for implementing strategy, text & cases.* Upper Saddle River, NJ: Prentice Hall.
2. Neely, A., ed. (2000). *Performance measurement—past, present and future.* Cranfield, United Kingdom: Centre for Business Performance, Cranfield University.
3. Vagneur, K., and M. Peiperl (2000). "Reconsidering performance evaluative style." *Accounting, Organisations and Society* 25, referring to: Argyris, C. (1952). *The impact of budgets on people.* The Controllership Foundation, Cornell University.
4. Kaplan, R. S., and D. P. Norton (1996). *The balanced scorecard: Translating strategy into action.* Boston: Harvard Business School Press.
5. Lipe, M. G., and S. E. Salterio (2000). "The balanced scorecard: Judgmental effects of common and unique performance measures." *Accounting Review* 75, 3:283–298.
6. Malina, M. A., and F. M. Selto (2000). *Communicating and controlling strategy: An empirical study of the effectiveness of the balanced scorecard.* Paper presented at the AAA Annual Conference, Philadelphia, August 13–16.

Part One

BEHAVIORAL FACTORS

1

BRIEF HISTORY OF PERFORMANCE MANAGEMENT SYSTEMS

In this chapter, the history and the developments of performance management systems are examined, and the importance of behavioral factors for the design, implementation, and use of performance management systems is established.

PURPOSE OF PERFORMANCE MANAGEMENT SYSTEMS

To be successful in the long run, an organization needs a clear and explicit management concept that is formulated by top management. This management concept is the basis for long-term development of the organizational strategy and strategic objectives. The strategy has to be translated at the lower levels of the organization into business unit plans, budgets, and operational action plans. The management concept must be supported through an unambiguous and well-organized planning and control cycle. This cycle gives clear feedback on the execution of the plans, using a so-called management control and information system. Having an effective planning and control cycle and management control and information system is critical for business success.

A management control and information system helps managers influence other members of an organization in such a way that the organization's mission and strategy are implemented, while simultaneously ensuring that resources are used effectively and efficiently.[1] A modern management control and information system distinguishes two components: (1) the management control structure, which states what the sys-

3

tem is; and (2) the management control process, which is what the system does (Exhibit 1.1).

The management control structure is defined as a combination of organizational activities (consisting of product–market combinations derived from the strategy), organizational structure (consisting of the division of authorities and responsibilities), standards of performance measurement and evaluation, infrastructure for the planning and control cycle, and infrastructure for management information. The management control process is defined as the steps and decisions taken when setting targets, allocating resources, evaluating performance, executing corrective actions, and realizing targets. Finally, the manner in which the man-

Exhibit 1.1 **Relationship Between Mission and Strategy of an Organization and Its Management Control Structure and Process**

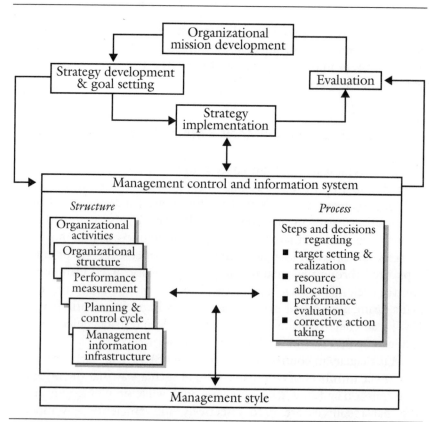

Source: Based on Petri, R., and G. J. A. M. van der Vossen (1994). "Management control structure." *Handbook Management Accounting*, D1100:1–33.

agement control system is used by an organization is referred to as the organization's management style.

Management control process, structure, and style have to be formulated and organized in such a way that the realization of targets of every organizational entity and the organization as a whole is supported and advanced. For this purpose, the management control and information system needs to provide adequate management information.

Four categories of management information use can be distinguished: (1) scorecard keeping, usually a standardized reporting process, which is characterized by consistency between time periods so comparisons are easy to make; (2) improving, understanding, and consequently problem solving; (3) focusing organizational attention and learning; and (4) legitimizing decisions.[2] *Performance* management information is specifically intended to be used to support decision-making processes to control the organization (and not decision-making processes in general). The effectiveness of performance management information is related to its contribution to the performance of the organization (and not only to the satisfaction of the user of the information). In order to obtain performance management information, performance measurement has to take place.

Performance measurement is defined in the management literature as "the process of quantifying past action, in which measurement is the process of quantification and past action determines current performance. Organizations achieve their goals by satisfying their customers with greater efficiency and effectiveness than their competitors. Effectiveness refers to the extent to which customer requirements are met and efficiency is a measure of how economically the organization's resources are utilized when providing a given level of customer satisfaction. A performance measure can now be defined as a metric used to quantify the efficiency and/or effectiveness of a past action."[3]

However, the term *measurement* is not quite correct because the process of performance measurement does not automatically lead to performance improvements. It should always initiate action through the use of appropriate measures. For this reason, performance *management* and performance *management* system are considered better terms. A performance management system is defined as "the formal, information-based routines and procedures managers use to maintain or alter patterns in organizational activities. These systems focus on conveying financial and nonfinancial information that influence decision making and managerial action taking. The recording, analyzing, and distributing of this information is embedded in the rhythm of the organization and is often based on predetermined practices and at preset times in the business cycle. These systems are designed specifically to be used by managers."[4]

A performance management system has many aims and purposes: helping to achieve sustainable improvements in organizational performance; acting as a lever for change in developing a more performance-oriented culture; increasing the motivation and commitment of employees; enabling individuals to develop their abilities, increase their job satisfaction, and achieve their full potential to their own benefit and that of the organization as a whole; enhancing the development of team cohesion and performance; developing constructive and open relationships between individuals and their managers in a process of continuing dialogue that is linked to the work actually being done throughout the year; providing opportunities for individuals to express their aspirations and expectations about their work; creating continuous improvement; supporting planning of organizational activities; reinforcing management rhetoric; introducing pay for group performance; influencing employees' attitudes; performing benchmarks; introducing individual and organizational learning; and focusing and justifying investments.[5]

After studying these aims and purposes, it can be noted that the use of a performance management system, in the context of the manager's work environment, resembles the planning and control cycle. The planning stage of the cycle starts after the long-term strategic objectives of the organization have been formulated and the corresponding management information needs have been defined. The purpose of this stage is to translate strategic plans into tangible, short-term action plans for each business unit. Management has at its disposal the results of the previous period(s) and the analysis of these results. These are used to make an action plan for the next period. It is crucial for people to use the analysis of the preceding period to learn from incorrect assessments or mistakes. Managers make use of a performance management system in the planning stage if: (1) they take the performance management system analysis of the preceding period as the basis for setting financial and nonfinancial targets for the next period(s); (2) they set priorities for the targets because these can be conflicting; (3) they determine which specific actions have to be taken to achieve these targets; (4) they allocate resources on the basis of planned actions and targets; and (5) they discuss the action planning with superiors and colleagues.

Making action plans is followed by implementing these plans. The manager has to make sure that this is done efficiently. The primary task of the manager in the control stage, therefore, is to communicate clearly the strategy, targets, and planned actions to all employees and to control their implementation. Additionally, the manager indicates which indicators need to be measured and the way in which this should be done. Managers make use of a performance management system in the control stage if they inform employees through the performance management system about the strategy, targets, planned actions, and the results to be measured and reported, and if they motivate employees by regularly providing intermediate feedback via the performance management system on the organization's results.

The purpose of the measurement stage is to collect information on the results of activities so that management can determine if adjustment is required. The three basic steps in how people acquire and process information are: (1) determination of information needs, (2) information seeking, and (3) information use—each of which can be considered in terms of cognitive, emotional, and situational factors.[6] Information needs arise when people experience cognitive gaps that hinder their progress and induce uncertainty. To bridge these gaps, they seek good, accessible information sources. During and after execution of activities, management makes sure that the organization's results are collected and recorded in the performance management system. The performance management system is used to provide feedback (via screens or reports) to managers on the implemented action plans. The feedback is closely studied by management to identify areas for improvement or correction. Managers make use of a performance management system in the measurement stage when they collect information in the performance management system for feedback purposes, study the results of the financial and nonfinancial targets and compare these with the budget, provide feedback via the performance management system to employees on the results and discuss these with them so that employees achieve the defined targets, and determine if there is a need for further analysis of the performance management system and which adjustments to the action plans are needed.

In the feedback stage, managers identify, based on the organization's results, those areas that need further attention and detailed interpretation. Managers look for causal relationships between the various results and try to find causes for lagging results in the internal and external environments. Feedback on the results to the employees and formulation and execution of corrective and preventive action then takes place. The performance management system is used to discuss frequently (mostly monthly) the execution and adjustment of action plans. In addition, the validity of the formulated strategy is discussed in periodic (less frequent, e.g., quarterly) meetings. Managers make use of a performance management system in the feedback stage if: (1) they interpret the key performance indicator (KPI) results and look for causal relationships between the different variables in the performance management system; (2) they look into the internal and external environments for explanations for lagging results and then formulate corrective actions on the basis of this analysis; (3) they discuss the information in the performance management system and possible adjustments to the action plans with colleagues; (4) they discuss the validity of the formulated strategy and check the underlying assumptions in quarterly meetings; (5) they share the information in the performance management system and the outcomes of periodic meetings with superiors and colleagues, thereby advising superiors about possible adjustments of strategic programs; and (6) they record important data from the discussions as well as of the outcomes of review and analysis meetings in the performance management system for future use and learning.

There are three key questions that must be answered when implementing a performance management system[7]:

1. *How can performance be measured in practice?* One has to look, among other things, at the definition of *results* and *result areas,* the validity of performance measures and indicators, and coverage of all relevant aspects.
2. *How involved are managers in a performance management system?* Under which conditions are managers willing to adapt a new system? This question is very relevant for the design of a performance management system because the purpose of this system is designed to influence managerial behavior.
3. *Have actual performance improvements been accomplished?* This is all about the tools and information managers need to be able to achieve quality improvements in their products and services.

To be able to answer the first question, we review in this chapter the history of performance management systems: the decline of the traditional management control and information system and the rise of a performance management system that is based on critical success factors (CSFs), KPIs, and the balanced scorecard (BSC). In addition, we look at the financial benefits and performance improvements an organization can expect from implementing such a performance management system, according to the literature. In Chapter 2, we turn to behavioral factors that are important for the design, implementation, and use of a performance management system that is based on CSFs, KPIs, and the BSC.

DEVELOPMENT OF PERFORMANCE MANAGEMENT SYSTEMS

Three stages can be distinguished in the development of management control and information systems, or performance management systems.[8] These stages are closely linked to industrial developments:

- *Stage 1: Very low system complexity.* Many of the earliest managed business organizations limited their attention to coordinating and controlling labor-intensive tasks in a few closely linked manufacturing processes that tended to produce fairly homogeneous product lines. Management control and information systems mainly focused on the collection of financial and nonfinancial data about efficiency of input and output conversion activities in processes, including nonaccounting data about cost of process outputs. Nineteenth-century firms measured their costs and revenues meticulously. However, they were careful to disclose very little information and often told their shareholders nothing about their performance.

- *Stage 2: Medium to high system complexity.* By the late nineteenth century, large-scale organizations integrated mass production with mass marketing and spanned a complex variety of intermediate and finished products. Frederick Taylor's scientific management was introduced around 1911, when it was argued that division and specialization of labor would lead to greater productivity. Standard production methods were used and standard costing techniques applied. In the period of 1920–1925, DuPont and General Motors experimented by introducing decentralized divisional structures with profit centers. As support for these reorganizations they also introduced the DuPont chart, and with it, the concept of return on investment (ROI). This meant that management was now also held responsible for the achievement of budgeted ROI, and therefore, not only focused on measures of margin and net income but also on return on investment.

- *Stage 3: Growing system complexity.* Between the 1920s and the 1980s, large business organizations had to cope with growing organizational complexity. They focused internal activities along product lines or geographic regions by creating multidivisional structures. Also, they increasingly decoupled functions and processes. This meant that the DuPont chart and the concept of ROI was used more and more. The principles of capital investment appraisal, budgeting, performance measurement, variance accounting, and ROI were introduced in the 1920s. By the 1930s, fully integrated cost and management accounting systems were developed, regulated, subjected to independent auditing, and linked to external financial operating systems. After the 1950s, management information systems focused on the growing use of accounting targets to control operating processes.

It can be stated that by the 1930s most standard cost accounting methods, such as budgeting, standard costing, transfer pricing, and the DuPont chart, had been developed and incorporated in the accounting textbooks. Only in sporadic instances were new developments, such as the concepts of residual income and net present value, included in the textbooks. However, after World War II, it became increasingly apparent that management needed other information than that supplied by the traditional management control and information systems. This information was needed because the systems and procedures of cost accounting and managerial control in use at that time were devised for manufacturing organizations with mass production. In this type of organization, cost–price calculation and responsibility accounting systems mainly focused on recording labor costs and minimizing manufacturing costs. In the 1980s, the competitive environment changed dramatically through the appearance of new technologies, increased competition as a consequence of deregulations, and the emergence of foreign producers. Quality improvements, reduced inventory, more efficient production processes, and increased automation were needed to face this new environment. These changes reduced the direct and indirect labor content of products and services and increased overhead costs. The traditional management accounting and information systems were not suited for modern organizations that were characterized by customer specific production, short life cycles, computer-aided design/computer-aided manufacturing technology and (more) overhead, creating many problems. Among the most frequent occurring problems, many of which endure well into the twenty-first century, are:

■ *One-sided information.* Management information is too financially oriented. This is caused by the fact that the management control and information systems have been designed to satisfy legal requirements. This means that the decision process is mainly based on financial measurements. Financial ratios, like ROI and working capital, are not used much. Nonfinancial information remains all too often restricted to personnel (number of full-time equivalents, absenteeism), project (i.e., status of large investments), and external (market share) information. Information about client satisfaction, vendor performance, innovation, product quality, and intellectual capital is insufficient or not available. The information is mainly internally focused on the activities of the organization itself. Information on competitors and environmental conditions is missing. Financial and nonfinancial targets are based on experiences in the past, not on client information or benchmark data. Information is often aimed at measuring the inputs, not the outputs. This focuses management on acquiring budgets instead of on the results that should be obtained by these budgets.

■ *Low-quality information.* Management reports are often incomplete, causing many requests from management for additional information. The information is too aggregated. End results are measured, but not the processes causing these results. The management control and information system is often not linked to the supplying operational systems, causing much manual work to generate reports. Many managers do not use the reporting possibilities of the operational and management control and information systems adequately.

■ *Tardy information.* Management information is too historically focused. Accurate measurement of past performance takes place, but forecasts of future performance are hardly made. This causes short-term behavior, going for the quick wins, instead of for long-term development and investment. The information is not supplied in appropriate time to management. Consequently, the value of the information decreases because necessary corrective actions are taken too late and the positive effects of these actions are delayed. Reports are still distributed in paper format, taking a long time. Another issue in this respect is that actions with a long-term effect are not executed because they negatively effect the short-term financial result.

■ *Misaligned organizational concept.* Management control and information systems are often based on outdated organizational concepts. They have been devised for manufacturing companies, while nowadays many organizations are predominantly service providers. To deal with these changes, many systems have been adjusted to reflect these changed circumstances, making them increasingly difficult to maintain and support. Critical business processes and functions are inadequately supported and measured. The execution of the organizational strategy is not measured adequately at all levels of the organization.

■ *Overload of data.* Management information does not contain ratios, trends, indicators, graphs, colors, and standardized layouts. The management control and information systems generate too much data. Conventional wisdom suggests that more data and more analysis lead to better decisions. However, research on information and decision making indicates that more is not always better. Also, the quality of analyses is low. Often, the figures are restated in text without giving an analysis of the real causes of the results. As a consequence, formulated actions cannot be effective because they do not address the real problems. Usually, the impact of these actions are not predicted either, so the organization has no idea of the effectiveness of its action. This all decreases the user friendliness and effectiveness of information.

- *Lack of communication.* Communication about management information is not structured, causing insufficient discussions and action on organizational results. Reports are rarely used for communicating (strategic) results to the organization.
- *Misaligned culture.* A culture of trust and continuous improvement does not exist in the organization, causing inadequate action on measured results. Because the wrong things are measured, the management accounting and information systems foster the wrong behavior. After all, "what gets measured gets managed." The systems do not take into account the mental images of managers toward information, causing a mismatch between the delivered information and the information managers actually want.

Many of these problems are caused by organizations using management control and information systems that are basically the same as those that existed in the 1930s. However, in the last few decades a constant stream of new developments in production and processing techniques—such as flexible manufacturing systems, just-in-time production, materials requirements planning, enterprise requirements planning, supply chain management, and total quality assurance—has been matched by new management information and accounting techniques such as target costing, value engineering, strategic cost accounting, activity-based costing/management, kaizen costing, and nonfinancial performance indicators. Although many of these new accounting techniques are variations of older methods and ideas, they nonetheless provide a valuable contribution to managing an increasingly complex environment.

The idea of nonfinancial measures in itself was not new. In the 1950s, General Electric implemented a balanced set of performance measures. In 1961, research showed that many organizations were "plagued by a common problem: inadequate management information, not in the sense of there not being enough, but in terms of relevancy for setting objectives, for shaping alternative strategies, for making decisions, and for measuring results against planned goals."[9] It was proposed that an organization needed a combination of environmental, competitive, and internal information provided by financial and nonfinancial data. That idea did not really catch on; not in the literature or in the practice of the day can much reference be found to nonfinancial indicators. This was probably because the idea was too optimistic about the capabilities of computers of that time to deliver the right information. The result was that significant improvements in the delivery of management information failed to materialize.

Then, in 1979, a study described a new approach to improve management control and information systems.[10] It proposed a concept called CSFs: "Critical success factors thus are, for any business, the limited number of areas in which results, if they are satisfactory, will ensure successful competitive performance for the organization. They are the few key areas where things must go right for the business to flourish. If results in these areas are not adequate, the organization's efforts for the period will be less than desired. As a result, the critical success factors are areas of activity that should receive constant and careful management attention. The current status of performance in each area should be continually measured and that information should be made available." These CSFs should, according to the study, be measured with prime measures, in later publications referred to as KPIs.

A CSF is defined as a qualitative description of an element of the strategy in which the organization has to excel in order to be successful. The CSF is made quantifiable with a KPI. The use of CSFs and KPIs enables measurement and, thus, control of strategic objectives. If performance indicators that measure the execution of the strategy and the creation of value to the organization are not included in the performance management process, it will not be transparent whether or not strategic objectives and value creation are being achieved. Exhibit 1.2 gives an example of a CSF and its KPIs.

Providing good customer service is of critical importance for an organization's success. One of the ways to provide this service is by increasing the focus on the customer throughout the organization, thereby increas-

Exhibit 1.2   CSF and Its Corresponding KPIs Example

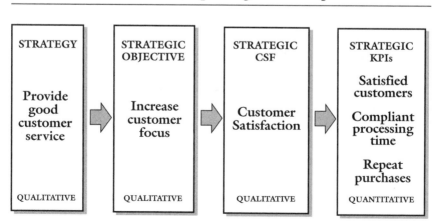

STRATEGY	STRATEGIC OBJECTIVE	STRATEGIC CSF	STRATEGIC KPIs
Provide good customer service	Increase customer focus	Customer Satisfaction	Satisfied customers Compliant processing time Repeat purchases
QUALITATIVE	QUALITATIVE	QUALITATIVE	QUANTITATIVE

ing customer satisfaction. Whether customer service is satisfactory is reflected in the number of customers that repeatedly buy products or services (i.e., repeat purchases). Customer satisfaction can also be measured by proactively asking customers what they think of the services provided (i.e., satisfied customers). An important activity that helps to keep customers satisfied is to respond quickly to complaints (i.e., complaint processing time).

It seemed the CSF concept initially caught on. At the time, CSFs were seen as a breakthrough approach to help executives focus on a few simple areas that were critical in the attainment of larger organizational goals. The theme, therefore, was quickly picked up by other researchers. However, after the initial surge of interest, it once again became rather quiet on the implementation front because managers were searching for even more simplified ways to represent cause–effect relationships at companies. This relative silence lasted until the beginning of the 1990s. At that time, Eccles published an important article in the *Harvard Business Review,* in which he predicted that a performance measurement revolution would take place in the next five years.[11] During this revolution, traditional financial information systems would be replaced by nonfinancial information systems. According to Eccles, this revolution was needed to improve managers' satisfaction with the information they receive, and to satisfy the increased information requirements of modern-day organizations caused by new techniques like total quality management, focus on customer satisfaction, and benchmarking.

Kaplan and Norton extended the CSF concept by introducing the concept of the BSC through a series of articles in the *Harvard Business Review* and books.[12] The BSC is used to represent the financial and non-financial performance indicators in a user-friendly format. Traditionally, a BSC has four perspectives or areas:

1. The *Innovation* perspective measures how often an organization introduces new products, services, or (production) techniques. In this way, the organization makes sure it does not become complacent but continuously renews itself. Sometimes organizations include people aspects in this perspective. These are used to measure the well-being, commitment, and competence of people in the organization. People aspects measure cultural qualities like internal partnership, teamwork, and knowledge sharing, as well as aggregate individual qualities like leadership, competency, and use of technology.

2. The *Internal* (or *process*) perspective measures the effectiveness of the processes by which the organization creates value. It follows

the innovation perspective because value is generally created in the production of new products, services, and techniques. The contribution of innovative people to the ability of the organization to create value consists of implementing and managing effective processes. The internal perspective measures how effectively processes operate. It precedes the customer perspective because efficient processes make it possible for an organization to stay or become more competitive.

3. The *Customer* perspective measures performance in terms of how the customer experiences the value created by the organization. It follows the internal perspective because value created by processes is meaningful only when it is perceived by the customer as being valuable.

4. The *Financial* perspective measures the bottom line, such as growth, ROI, and the other traditional measures of business performance. It is the last perspective because it is the final result of good, committed people; of implementing and operating effective processes; of the ability for renewal; and of creating value that customers have chosen to purchase.

In different organizations, the perspectives and the leading indicators can be different, but the idea of the BSC is to provide a balanced set of measurements that allow an organization to measure the cause-and-effect chain by which customer and shareholder value is created. If value is created by people working on and in processes to satisfy customers and to produce financial results, then managers must be able to measure and monitor all of these perspectives of value creation to effectively manage the business. By combining lagging and leading CSFs and KPIs, managers gain an understanding of where the organization was and where it is going. The "balanced" in the BSC can be found in several aspects: Nonfinancial data complements financial data, leading information (customer and innovative data) complements lagging information (financial and internal data), and internal information (financial, internal, and innovative data) complements external information (customer data). Exhibit 1.3 gives an example of the BSC.

The main benefit of managing with a combination of financial and nonfinancial information is that the use of leading, nonfinancial indicators facilitates proactive control and the ability to take preventive action. A balanced set of key financial and nonfinancial CSFs and KPIs enables management to focus on the really important issues that drive business performance and to monitor the achievement of strategic goals more closely. Using nonfinancial information improves the analysis capabilities

Exhibit 1.3   **BCS Example**

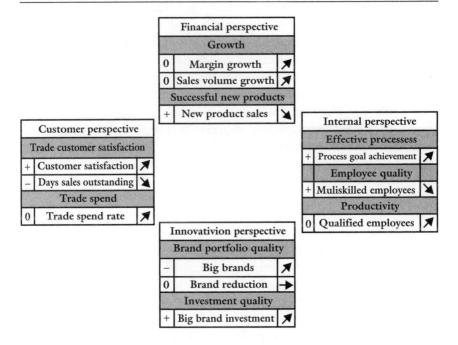

of managers because they can identify the root causes of financial performance. The nonfinancials can include external information, making it possible for management to compare the internal results with external trends and drivers.

It is interesting to see how Kaplan and Norton extended ideas proposed earlier by other authors. For instance, their lagging and leading indicators were mentioned by Rockart as monitoring and building CSFs. A well-known predecessor of the BSC is the Tableau de Bord. It emerged in France at the end of the nineteenth century, having been developed by process engineers who were looking for ways to improve the production process by understanding better the cause–effect relationships. The same principle was then applied at the top management level to give senior management a set of indicators that would allow them to monitor progress of the business, compare it to the goals that had been set, and give them the corrective actions needed. Each organizational unit had its own Tableau de Bord, which was not limited to financial indicators but extended with operational measures. Just as the BSC, the development of the Tableau de Bord involved translating an organizational unit's vision and mission into a set of objectives, from which the unit identified its CSFs that then were translated into a series of quantitative KPIs. To provide managers with the information they could use for decision making, the Tableau de Bord primarily contained performance indicators that largely were controllable by the organizational unit.

Many management writers and the business community at large firmly believe that the BSC is here to stay, mainly because the BSC is "an idea whose time has come" due to the growing frustration with traditional measurement systems, coupled with an increasing need to cope with an ever more complex world. The concept is also extremely well packaged and has been carefully marketed. Finally, the concept is easy to comprehend, which means that people reading about the BSC for the first time can immediately understand it.

This does not mean that the BSC is without weaknesses. One weakness is the emphasis on the customer perspective, implicitly ignoring the broader market perspective, which concentrates on how the organization looks to the customer in comparison with competitors. A second weakness of the BSC is the absence of any mention of suppliers. It is assumed that if the business itself excels, then all will be well, but in these days of increased outsourcing, business interdependencies are continually growing. Some organizations have had bad experiences with BSC implementations, in which they have abandoned their scorecards after a few years without consistent results or as a result of difficulties during the implementation phase. These organizations have reported problems in defining the measures, especially in areas where performance is more qualitative than quantitative, and in decomposing the measures to lower levels in the organizations. A final criticism of the BSC is the disregard for the human element, that is, the effect a BSC can have on managerial attitudes or the question of whether a BSC is suitable for every type of manager.

The developments in the field of performance management systems can be summarized as:

- *Organizations pay more attention to the design of the performance management system.* Until recently, many organizations would, while setting up a new performance management system, automatically have designed *ROI* criteria and deviation analyses without really looking at the effectiveness of these indicators. Nowadays, the choice of KPIs comes from a structured process, in which the strategy and CSFs of an organization take a central place.
- *Organizations broaden the CSF/KPI set in the performance management system.* In addition to the traditional financial indicators, CSFs and KPIs are now included in management reporting to monitor strategic goals like quality, delivery time, client satisfaction, competitor ranking, and employee retention.

- *Organizations go from absolute to relative KPIs and from separate indicators to a coherent set of indicators.* In the past, absolute targets were set for the KPIs that had to be achieved, no matter what. Nowadays, striving for continuous improvement causes targets to be changed regularly in an upward direction. The links between KPIs are also made more visible, and the KPIs are put in a balanced measurement system.

Why does the performance management system, based on CSFs, KPIs, and the BSC, now experience a breakthrough? One reason can be the recent developments in the area of information technology. Introducing CSFs, KPIs, and the BSC requires collecting, storing, and reporting a lot of new data. In the 1990s, an increasing number of software vendors came to market with special applications called executive information systems (EISs), which could better support the data and reporting requirements of CSFs and KPIs. These new applications, combined with dramatically improved price–performance ratios in hardware and breakthroughs in software and database technology, made it possible for organizations to generate, disseminate, analyze, and store more information from more sources for more people more quickly and cheaply than ever before. With modern database technology, it is now possible to analyze information in a number of different ways and in effect to have different information systems for different purposes. In general, it can be stated that information is becoming more widely dispersed throughout the organization. Databases can be accessed through corporate networks, so that anybody within the organization can have easy access to the information database. This means that a manager with a PC on his desk can very easily access a whole range of corporate information, including accounting information. This has led to a decentralization of information.

Another reason for the final breakthrough is that due to the emphasis on total quality management (TQM) these last few decades, the significance of performance measurement did not really get highlighted until recent years. Organizations are just now realizing that they need to quantify the benefits of TQM by providing management information that clearly demonstrates its credibility as a concept.

A third reason can be found in the changing nature of the economy. In the traditional economy, which is dominated by tangible assets, financial measurements are adequate to record investments and expenses associated with inventory, property, and plant and equipment. However, in the new economy, in which intangible assets have become the major sources of competitive advantage, information tools are needed that describe knowledge-based assets and the value-creating strategies that these assets make possible. A 1982 Brookings Institute study that showed that tangible book values represented 62% of industrial organizations' market values, while 10 years later this ratio had dropped to 38%.[13] Later studies estimated that by the end of the twentieth century, the book value of tangible assets accounted only for 10 to 15% of companies' market values. It can be concluded that a different kind of management information is needed, like the BSC, to capture the move that has taken place in the main sources of creating value. These are shifting from managing tangible assets to managing knowledge-based strategies that deploy an organization's intangible assets—customer relationships; innovative products and services; high-quality and responsive operating processes; information technology and databases; and employee capabilities, skills, and motivation.

This time the concept of performance indicators indeed seems here to stay: The introduction of nonfinancial performance measures is not a passing fad. This is because the size and scale of today's organizational operations are so complex that no chief executive officer (CEO) possesses the level of knowledge needed to manage all the company's operations and people. Consequently, today's CEO must incorporate additional sources of information in the decision-making process. What makes a further difference is that the combination of a strong, appealing concept developed by leading business school professors and the availability of supporting technology seems to be so appealing that many organizations decide to (finally) accept CSFs and KPIs. Maybe the rapid adaptation of the BSC by managers and consultants can be viewed as evidence that the revolution predicted by Eccles is indeed under way.

BENEFITS OF PERFORMANCE MANAGEMENT SYSTEMS

Applying CSFs, KPIs, and the BSC has a number of benefits, many of which address the problems encountered with the traditional management control and information systems as described in the previous section. These advantages are:

■ *Better quality of information.* CSFs and KPIs support effective planning and budgeting processes because they make the relationship between functions and activities on the one hand and performance on the other hand more clear. Reports are more complete and give a better view of crucial business activities. CSFs and KPIs translate organizational strategy into qualitative and quantitative measures on all management levels. Through this, the execution of the strategy can be continuously measured and adjusted. This alignment will result in higher organizational performance.

- *Timeliness of information.* When things go wrong, CSFs and KPIs function as an early warning system, giving signals about potential issues before these actually happen or become real (comprehensive) problems. Managers can, therefore, better anticipate new developments because they receive better information at an earlier stage, thereby significantly lowering the chance that the problems really become life threatening for the organization. Interesting to note is that a study of the key strategies of Europe's most successful companies found that managers of these organization used action-oriented philosophies to add value and that they do so within the shortest possible time frames.[14]

- *Better support of management.* CSFs and KPIs make the concepts of continuous improvement and the learning organization possible, by focusing people's attention on continuous improvement and development, and by continuously raising performance expectations. Total quality management is enforced by ensuring that the expectations of external and internal customers drive the activities and performance of the people in the organization. Because managers have a better insight into and a better grip on organizational performance, cost reduction, organizational improvements, product quality, and service improvements are made possible.

- *Better communication.* A set of clear CSFs and KPIs forms a common basis for communication and discussion in the organization. This makes information transferable between departments and organizational units, making information less prone to being used as a means of executing power.

- *Aligned culture.* The availability of high-quality information at all management levels makes management by delegation possible, which speeds up the decision-making process. Better reporting enhances managers' self-management and self-control. People are more motivated because their goals and what is expected from them in regard to their behavior and performance is clear, and they get regular feedback on how they are doing in these respects. The culture of an organization is impacted because the performance management process ensures that consistency exists between what an organization says it values and what is actually measured and rewarded. Also, information is more standardized, providing a better basis for discussion at all levels of the organization.

Managers are constantly under pressure to measure the performance of their organization, but there is little empirical evidence about the impact of such measurement on performance. On the one hand, the link between organizational effectiveness and performance measures has been widely recognized. On the other hand, explanations for this link are constrained by the lack of clear theoretical foundations to many measurement tools and techniques and an apparent preference for description and prescription on the part of writers in the field. Some studies do not find a clear link between the use of nonfinancial measures and organizational performance. This could be caused by the fact that organizations might consider changes to the performance management system less important than organizational structural arrangements or that the main benefits of increasing the use of nonfinancial measures is more motivational rather than instrumental, or that performance is a complex variable with a multiplicity of factors contributing to the level of global performance at any point in time. It is often easier to prove reverse causation: "We know that you cannot prove that X produces Y, but neither can you prove that it did not. For example, when a study claims to establish that there is a proven connection between performance management and measures of organizational performance, it is a matter of speculation as to whether the results in the most effective companies were created by performance management or whether the most effective companies were the ones most likely to introduce performance management."[15]

Nonetheless, an increasing body of anecdotal evidence can be found about the positive relation between the use of a performance management system, based on CSFs, KPIs, and the BSC, and the performance of the organization. According to the Institute of Management Accountants (IMA), some of the best companies in the world, such as AT&T, Bell-South, Bristol-Myers Squibb, Dun & Bradstreet, DuPont, Emerson Electric, General Electric, Hewlett-Packard, Johnson & Johnson, Merck, Motorola, Pepsico, Wal-Mart, and Xerox cite their integrated performance management system as one of the key drivers of their success.[16] The general tendency in the literature seems to be that organizations that have implemented and are using a performance management system perform better financially as well as nonfinancially than those organizations that are less performance management driven. This is explained by the fact that performance measures direct attention and motivate the organization to act in a strategically desirable way. They also help management to assess progress toward strategic goals. Finally, performance measures help an individual to see his or her part in the wider enterprise with greater clarity.

The case of Sears, Roebuck shows that the nonfinancial indicator "employee loyalty" is related to customer satisfaction, which in turn is related to organization's growth and profits.[17] Statistical analysis of sales data at Sears, Roebuck showed that employee attitudes drive both customer satisfaction and changes in revenue. A 5% improvement in employee attitude results in a 1.3% improvement in customer satisfaction, which in turn results in a 0.5% increase in store revenue. Independent surveys showed that national retail customer satisfaction had fallen for several years, but in the time period for which the data was analyzed, employee satisfaction at Sears had risen by 4%, and customer satisfaction by almost 4%. This translated into more than $200 million in additional revenues for that year and increased Sears's market capitalization at that time by nearly one quarter of a billion dollars.

In a research study, senior executives from 58 organizations with a performance management system in place and operational that focused on measuring a set of financial and nonfinancial data were asked how their organizations were ranked compared to their peers in the industry.[18] The same question was asked of senior executives from 64 organizations without such a performance management system. The executives' opinions—1,000 in all—were juxtaposed with the three-year ROI of their organizations (Exhibit 1.4).

In this same study, it was observed that companies with a balanced performance management system, compared to their peers, displayed a number of cultural differences that are summarized in Exhibit 1.5.

Exhibit 1.4   **Relationship Between Performance Management and Organizational Performance**

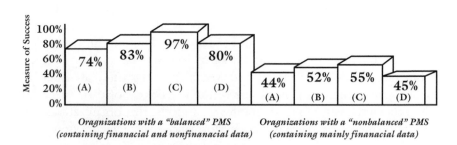

(A) Perceived as an industry leader over the past 3 years
(B) Reported to be financially ranked in the top 3 of their industry
(C) Last major cultural or operational change judged to be very or moderately successful
(D) Three year ROI

Source: Schiemann, W. A., and J. H. Lingle (1999). *Bullseye! Hitting your strategic targets through high-impact measurement.* New York: The Free Press.

Exhibit 1.5 **Organizations with Different Performance Management Systems Exhibit Different Cultures**

Indicator of Organizational Success	*Organizations with a Balanced Performance Management System (%)*	*Organizations with a Nonbalanced Performance Management System (%)*
Clear agreement on strategy among senior management	93	37
Good cooperation and teamwork among management	85	38
Unit performance measures are linked to strategic company measures	74	16
Information within the organization is shared openly and candidly	71	30
Effective communication of strategy to organization	60	8
Willingness by employees to take risks	52	22
Individual performance measures are linked to unit measures	52	11
High levels of self-monitoring of performance by employees	42	16

Source: Schiemann, W. A., and J. H. Lingle (1999). *Bullseye! Hitting your strategic targets through high-impact measurement.* New York: The Free Press.

Exhibit 1.6 **Comparison of Organizations with a Structured or an Unstructured Performance Management System**

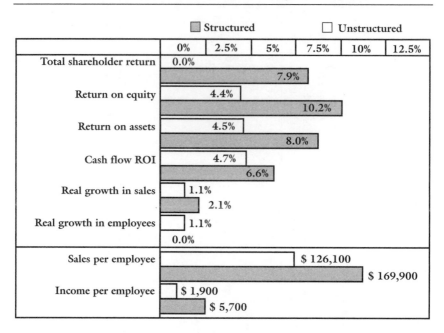

	Structured	Unstructured

	0%	2.5%	5%	7.5%	10%	12.5%
Total shareholder return	0.0%					
				7.9%		
Return on equity		4.4%				
					10.2%	
Return on assets		4.5%				
				8.0%		
Cash flow ROI		4.7%				
			6.6%			
Real growth in sales	1.1%					
	2.1%					
Real growth in employees	1.1%					
	0.0%					
Sales per employee				$ 126,100		
					$ 169,900	
Income per employee	$ 1,900					
	$ 5,700					

In another study, the performance management processes and financial results of 437 publicly traded firms were studied.[19] Of the sample, 232 companies said they did not use a structured performance management system to continuously provide the organization with data about the performance of their employees but instead conducted only year-end evaluations or no evaluations at all. The other 205 companies said they did use a performance management system. The study looked at the three-year financial performance of these companies, showing a strong favorable result for the organizations with a structured performance management system (Exhibit 1.6).

In the same study, the average changes in financial ratios, before and after implementing a structured performance management system, provides evidence in favor of implementing a structured performance management system (Exhibit 1.7).

In yet another study, personnel managers from organizations with a process to structurally and continuously measure the performance of managers and employees were asked how effective this performance management system was in improving the overall performance of their organizations (Exhibit 1.8).[20] The majority of the respondents graded the effectiveness of the performance management system positively. This effectiveness was especially found in the achievement of financial targets,

Exhibit 1.7   **Changes in Financial Performance, Before and
After Implementing a Structured Performance
Management System**

Financial Ratio	Average Before	Average After	Average Change
Total shareholder return	− 5.1%	19.7%	24.8%
Stock return (relative to market index)	− 0.13%	0.18%	0.31%
Price/book value of total capital	0.03%	0.26%	0.23%
Real value/cost	− 0.06	0.13	0.19
Sales per employee ($1,000)	98.8	193.0	94.2

Source: Gubman, E. L. (1998). *The talent solution: Aligning strategy and people to achieve extraordinary results.* New York: McGraw-Hill.

development of skills and competencies, and improved customer care and process quality. The conclusion of the study was that the majority of the people polled believed it was well worth the effort and expense to install a performance management system.

A study performed by a consultancy firm showed that the majority of the interviewed organizations with a high financial return (measured in margin and profit) turned out to have a performance management system that contained financial as well as nonfinancial information, with an emphasis on exception reporting, and a strong focus on client satisfaction and market indicators.[21] A study of Australian manufacturing firms found that financial performance measures continued to be an important aspect of the performance management system.[22] However, these were being supplemented with a variety of nonfinancial measures. From these, high

Exhibit 1.8   **Degree of Impact of the Performance Management
System on Organizational Performance**

Effectiveness of the Performance Management System	Percentage of Organizations
Very effective	7
Moderately effective	41
Slightly effective	29
Ineffective	8
Don't know/not stated	15

benefits were derived from customer satisfaction surveys and nonfinancial measures. Relatively moderate benefits were reported for ongoing supplier evaluations, BSCs, qualitative measures, and team performance measures.

An interesting sideline is that it seems that major investors' decisions are significantly influenced by nonfinancial performance information.[23] It turns out that over a third of the typical investor's allocation decisions is attributable not to the financials but to other information on performance areas perceived to be leading indicators of future profitability. These include perceptions of a company's strategic vision and the company's ability to execute it, the credibility of management, the prospects of innovations in the pipeline, the ability to attract talented people, and so on. It was found that those analysts who rely heavily on nonfinancial information are the ones producing the most accurate earnings forecasts. The major implication of this is that if a firm does not strategically manage, measure, and communicate about key areas of nonfinancial performance, its operating performance and the value of its securities can suffer. This result is also found for the relation between customer satisfaction measures and organizational performance and stock market performance.

In a survey conducted by the IMA, 40% of the respondents said they were in the process of changing their performance management system.[24] Of these, approximately 70% describe the change as a "major overhaul" or "replacement" of the performance management system. The BSC framework was reported as gaining support at many companies. Bain & Company was quoted to estimate that 55% of the U.S. companies they surveyed and 45% of the European companies used the BSC. According to the survey, approximately 40% of the respondents were currently using a BSC or planned to do so within the next year. Twelve percent of these companies had been using the BSC for more than two years with positive effects (Exhibit 1.9). In the survey, approximately 83% of the respon-

Exhibit 1.9 **Respondents Were Asked to Agree or Disagree with Statements About Their Performance Management System (1 = Strongly Disagree, 5 = Strongly Agree)**

Statement	BSC Users	Non-BSC Users
Our compensation/incentive programs are clearly tied to nonfinancial performance measurements	3.00	2.07
Our performance measurement system supports the corporate vision and strategies	3.31	2.83
There are clear linkages between performance measures in our performance measurement system	3.31	2.57

dents said that the BSC was worth implementing or "not yet, but will be"; the other 17% said "too early to tell."

Ten of the twelve companies that were the first users of the BSC were asked how they have done since the implementation of the BSC and what their experiences were.[25] Five of the companies reported their BSC implementation to be a "resounding success," measured either in financial or cultural terms. Clear differences were found among the 10 companies, which made it possible to divide them into two groups, each with distinct characteristics. One group mainly implemented the BSC to improve organizational performance in quantitative, financial terms (drive value). The other group focused on organizational performance improvement in qualitative, nonfinancial terms (drive values). The research results are summarized in Exhibit 1.10.

Exhibit 1.10 **Experience of the Original BSC Companies**

Question	"Drive Value" Organizations	"Drive Values" Organizations
Aim of scorecard	Drive financial success.	Effect cultural change.
Project approach	Explicit project, small team, proposal of measures, guide implementation.	Explicit project, small team, proposal of measures, guide implementation.
Layout and content of scorecard	Kaplan and Norton perspectives, with measures derived from the strategy.	Interactive process, based on a perceived, not a concise strategy, resulting in different number and sort of perspectives.
Sort of measures	Initially too many. Measures which are explicitly and quantifiably linked to the strategy. Nonfinancial measures that produce objective, accurate values. Index measures for trend analysis. Outcome measures.	Measures that "telegraph" what really matters to the organization's success. Outcome and activity measures.
Aggregation of measures	No, aggregation of financials obscure real performance. Seek or "logical" rather than arithmetic connection of division results to corporate performance.	No, aggregation of financials obscure real performance. Seek or "logical" rather than arithmetic connection of division results to corporate performance.

(continues)

ACTION:

Exhibit 1.10   **Continued**

Question	"Drive Value" Organizations	"Drive Values" Organizations
External disclosure of values	No, not yet. Legally too risky and investors look for other sources of nonfinancial information.	No, not yet. Legally too risky and investors look for other sources of nonfinancial information.
Link to individual pay	Yes, when previous performance management systems were already linked, otherwise no. If yes: specific linkages between pay and performance on the scorecard aspects.	Yes, when previous performance management systems were already linked, otherwise no. If yes: based on broadly based gain (and risk) sharing plans.
Replacement of old performance management systems	Many old measures are included (familiar, linked with human resource processes).	Many old measures are included (familiar, linked with human resource processes).
Resistance	Modest/evolutionary or full-scale replacement: little resistance.	Modest/evolutionary or full-scale replacement: little resistance.
Implementation worthwhile?	Half of the companies: "a resounding success." Bottom line has improved for some and for others not yet. Success in: ■ fundamentally changing the bottom line ■ focusing employee attention on strategic priorities and the leading indicators of financial success ■ new visibility and better management of the value chain	Half of the companies: "a resounding success." Bottom line has improved for some and for others not yet. Success in: ■ realizing substantive change in employee orientation and the corporate beliefs system ■ shift in organizational culture ■ employees better in prioritizing multiple change projects ■ boosts in employee morale, customer satisfaction, and product quality

In their latest book, Kaplan and Norton also revisit the pioneer organizations of the BSC. They report that these organizations "enjoyed substantial benefits from their new strategies early in their implementation activities." Examples are given of organizations going from years of below-average performance to first in their niche or industry in both growth and profitability, with the turnaround accomplished within two years of introducing a new strategy, a new organization, and the BSC performance management process. Kaplan and Norton argue that "the BSC made the difference. Each organization executed strategies using the same physical and human resources that had previously produced failing performance. The strategies were executed with the same products, the same facilities, the same employees, and the same customers. The difference was a new senior management team using the BSC to focus all organizational resources on a new strategy."[26]

All in all, the literature starts to give more proof that implementing a performance management system can yield many benefits also in financial terms. This gives a compelling argument for organizations to implement such a system.

ISSUES WITH CRITICAL SUCCESS FACTORS, KEY PERFORMANCE INDICATORS, AND THE BALANCED SCORECARD

One may wonder why, if there are so many advantages of using CSFs, KPIs, and the BSC, every organization has not yet implemented these. This could be because the implementation and use of these types of measures are not easy and require special knowledge and training. Another aspect can be that, as soon as performance measures are used as a means of control, the people whose indicators are tracked begin to manage the performance on their indicators instead of the performance on their activities. The problems mentioned in relation to CSFs, KPIs, and the BSC can be divided into five categories:

1. *Behavioral displacement.* The performance management system encourages behaviors that are not consistent with the organization's strategy and objectives. There are many examples of this. Managers pursue narrow local objectives, at the expense of the objectives of the organization as a whole *(suboptimization)*. On top of this, the priority areas of strategic importance to the organization to target for performance measurement systems may be strongly contested. Also, many outputs are the result of team rather than individual efforts. As a result, if the implicit reward scheme is directed at individuals, suboptimization can arise. There is an inherent trade-off between the beneficial incentive effects of

a formal control mechanism and the dysfunctional consequences of suboptimization. Managers pursue short-term targets at the expense of legitimate long-term objectives *(myopia)*. This is caused by the fact that performance indicators are imperfect reflections of the efficacy of current management because they can indicate the results of managerial endeavor over many years, and they cannot always reflect the future consequences of current managerial actions. The problem is exacerbated by the short-term career perspectives of many workers. Managers emphasize measures of success rather than the underlying objective *(measure fixation)*. If a measure does not fully capture all dimensions of the associated objective, managers may be encouraged to pursue strategies that enhance the reported measure rather than further the associated objective. Finally, management emphasizes phenomena that are quantified in the performance management system at the expense of nonquantifiable aspects of performance *(tunnel vision)*. Most organizations usually hold a large number of diverse objectives and it is often impractical or impossible to identify and track all of these objectives. It is impossible to devise a managerial reward scheme that satisfactorily reflects achievement in more than three or four dimensions. Also, specifically for the public sector, ramifications of public sector services extend well beyond the immediate target of service delivery.

2. *Gamesmanship.* Managers take actions that are intended to improve their performance indicators without producing any positive economic effects for the organization. Managers deliberately manipulate data so that reported behavior differs from actual behavior. For instance, by minimizing the apparent scope for productivity improvements, any reported improvement in one year will result in increased expectations (and targets) for future years. Gaming can come in the form of "creative reporting" and fraud. If excessive reliance is placed on KPIs to control the organization, there is clearly an incentive for managers to manipulate the data under their control to show their organization's performance in the most advantageous light *(misrepresentation)*. Also, managers can adjust their activities in such a way that measurements on irrelevant KPIs lead to satisfactory results. This misrepresentation of results might lead to misallocation of resources and inequitable treatment of staff and clients. Although in possession of all the facts, the manager might systematically misinterpret them and, thereby, send the wrong signals to the superior *(misinterpretation)*. This can be caused because the KPI reporting that is pro-

vided by the financial department is incomprehensible for managers. Also, evaluation of performance measurement activities is often constrained by a lack of understanding of causal links between performance measurement and performance improvement. Finally, top management does not use the BSC consistently and reverts back to discussing financial measures when things go bad *(regression)*. This happens in part due to their ability with financial measures.

3. *Operating delays.* These are caused by administrative and bureaucratic procedures installed to exercise control, like requiring an excessive number of signatures on a requisition form. These delays create frustration with and resistance to the performance management system. A special form of delay, called *inertia,* occurs when there is not enough attention for following up on the results on KPIs. Employees are not given (enough) feedback on their results and action is not taken on lagging results. There are no other control mechanisms in place which support the performance management system, such as human resources systems that reward good results on KPIs, accountability structures that make clear who is responsible for which KPIs, and a regular review of the quality of management in dealing with KPIs. Organizational paralysis is brought about by an excessively rigid system of evaluation, thus inhibiting innovation. This danger arises due to the inevitable delay in designing and putting in place an evaluation scheme and the effort required to change it subsequently.

4. *Negative attitudes.* The performance management system causes negative attitudinal effects like job tension, conflict, frustration, and resistance because managers do not want to feel controlled or think that the performance management system is not effective, sensible, or ethical. Managers object to being evaluated and judged by outsiders or other people in the organization *(clouding the transparency).* This is called "perceived reduction in autonomy." People object to sharing their knowledge of the processes they have been put in charge of. That is why they object to the KPIs, which make their performance transparent. In addition to this, managers constantly question the relevance of KPIs and also question the economical foundation of the KPI calculations *(beating the system).* They simply label the management information as "plainly wrong." Managers also state that the KPIs are not an accurate representation of their activities, that targets have been set in the wrong way, or that measuring nonfinancial indicators does not lead to increased profitability or growth. Many

times managers have developed their own sources of information. Also, selecting relevant and valid approaches that are also culturally and politically acceptable in the organization can be highly problematic *(cultural mismatch)*. Cultural barriers can exist, where organizations approach performance measurement based on tradition and the accepted way of doing things. These traditions or embedded cultural norms are formidable barriers to change and can cause many negative feelings.

5. *Structural deficits.* Development methods that work well in some organizations may fail to deliver in apparently similar organizations *(incompatibility)*. However, organizations cannot go from the assumption that implementation can take place with a standard approach, it will stay made to measure for each organization. In addition, the system can be(come) too complex with too many separate measures causing *indicator overload*. In general, people can keep only about seven things in their heads at any one time. This means that having many indicators dilutes the attention people can pay to any single issue or even a small set of issues. Structural deficits can already be created during the implementation phase, when the provision of resources (time, skill, and information) for systematic implementation is resisted from above and below and, consequently, is inadequate for the implementation project *(resource shortage)*. Apart from that, many organizations have a track record of starting and later abandoning initiatives such as the BSC. Many employees may have grown weary of such change efforts.

Many of the problems described above can be seen as "facts of organizational life," which are related to change management, culture, and power.[27] These may be addressed merely by acknowledging these issues and being sensitive to them when designing performance measurement systems, applying techniques that have established theoretical bases together with managerial flair. The problems reflect the natural evolutionary cycle that is at work in the development of theory and practice in the field of performance management systems. In the late 1980s and early 1990s, managers were concerned that they were measuring the wrong things, so they began to explore and then adopt new and alternative measurement frameworks, such as the BSC. Throughout the 1990s, they struggled to implement these measurement frameworks. Now the most advanced organizations appear to be asking the next question in this natural evolutionary cycle: how to use the data provided by the new systems.[28]

IMPORTANCE OF BEHAVIORAL FACTORS

The answer to the question of how to use the data provided by the new performance management system may very well lie with the system users themselves. A common thread through the issues described above seems to be the way a manager views information, uses information, and deals with other people while utilizing information. Management styles, like knowledge, skills, and individual motives and experiences, are important to the use of management information. Several authors state that at the heart of the problem of performance measurement is the human element, and that this element appears to be the "make or break" factor for success.[29] Performance management systems can, therefore, not be designed without taking into account human behavior, and the successful implementation of performance measurement approaches depends on understanding and accommodating the human element in performance measurement.

The fields of study called behavioral accounting and reliance on accounting performance measures (RAPM) concentrate on the behavioral and organizational effects of using accounting information for the performance evaluation of subordinate managers.[30] These also signify the extent to which superiors rely on and emphasize those performance criteria that are qualified in accounting and financial terms and are prespecified as budget targets. RAPM is a substantial departure from the mechanical approach to performance measurement found in traditional management theory. Through RAPM, the issue of the human element receives more attention in literature, although a lot of this attention is still focused on its relationship to the budgeting system.

Personality factors have been mentioned before in the literature as important determinants of management styles and attitudinal reactions to budgeting. For this reason, likely candidates for investigation are personality variables related to individual preferences for risk and uncertainty. Thus, it is well worth exploring individual psychological responses to performance assessment and the nature of the systemic effects created by other formal and informal management control processes, such as reward, planning, training, and information systems. This would require synthesis of two levels of analysis (individual and system) as well as consideration of psychology, organizational behavior, behavioral accounting, and systems theory research.

Performance management systems can incite managers to display counterproductive behavior because managers are often ignored when a new system is set up. For example, the design of most BSCs is predominantly determined by the characteristics of the organization and its strategy. The characteristics of performance management system users are generally not taken into account, although it would make sense to do so. The way managers handle information and their personalities could very well designate the design of the performance management system.

Special attention should then be paid to the behavioral issues surrounding the use of a performance management system. Unfortunately, there are not many concrete examples in the literature of the importance of the human element to the use of a performance management system. A reason for this lack may be the influence of the widely adopted definition of management control of Anthony.[31] Although Anthony specifically suggested that the study of control should be broadly based in the behavioral sciences, his work showed little evidence of borrowing from behavioral sciences. Consequently, control has popularly taken on the connotation of accounting control and the study of control systems has become overly narrow by remaining focused primarily upon accounting control mechanisms. Another reason may be that many organizations still operate using an oversimplified or incorrect model of human behavior, which has become institutionalized in certain types of measures and measurement systems. These systems have become a signal of competent management and are so widely diffused that firms are reluctant not to use them. However, I think that addressing these behavioral factors is crucial and beneficial for successful implementation and use of performance management systems.

ENDNOTES

1. Anthony, R. N., J. Dearden, and N. M. Bedford (1989). *Management control systems,* 6th ed. Chicago: Irwin.
2. Simon, H., H. Guetzkow, K. Kozmetsky, and G. Tyndall (1954). *Centralization vs. decentralization in organizing the controllers department.* Controllership Foundation paper; Vandenbosch, B. (1999). "An empirical analysis of the association between the use of executive support systems and perceived organizational competitiveness." *Accounting, Organizations and Society* 24:77–92.
3. Neely, A. (1998). *Measuring business performance: Why, what and how.* London: The Economist Books.
4. Simons, R. (2000). *Performance measurement and control systems for implementing strategy, text & cases.* Upper Saddle River, NJ: Prentice Hall.
5. Armstrong, M., and A. Baron (1998). *Performance management: The new realities.* London: Institute of Personnel and Development; Martins, R. A. (2000). "Use of performance measurement systems: Some thoughts

towards a comprehensive approach." In A. Neely, ed., *Performance measurement—past, present and future*. Cranfield, United Kingdom: Centre for Business Performance, Cranfield University, 363–370.

6. Choo, C. W. (2000). "Closing the cognitive gaps: How people process information." In Marchand, D. A., T. H. Davenport, and T. Dickson, eds., *Mastering information management: Complete MBA companion in information management*. Harlow: Prentice Hall Financial Times, 245–253.

7. Algera, J. A. (2000). "Performance management in organisaties, tien jaar ervaring met ProMES" (transl. Performance management in organizations, ten years of experience with ProMES). *Bedrijfskunde* 2:14–19.

8. Johnson, H. T., and R. S. Kaplan (1987). *Relevance lost: The rise and fall of management accounting*. Boston: Harvard Business School Press.

9. Daniel, D. R. (1961). "Management information crisis." *Harvard Business Review*. September/October, 111–121.

10. Rockart, J. F. (1979). "Chief executives define their own data needs." *Harvard Business Review*. March/April, 81–93.

11. Eccles, R. G. (1991). "The performance measurement manifesto." *Harvard Business Review*. January/February, 131–137.

12. Kaplan, R. S., and D. P. Norton (1992). "The balanced scorecard: Measures that drive performance." *Harvard Business Review*. January/February, 71–79; "Putting the balanced scorecard to work." *Harvard Business Review*. September/October; "Using the Balanced Scorecard as a Strategic Management System." *Harvard Business Review*. January/February, 75–85; *The balanced scorecard: Translating strategy into action*. Boston: Harvard Business School Press; *The strategy-focused organization: How balanced scorecard companies thrive in the new business environment*. Boston: Harvard Business School Press. Early indications for these works can be found in: Kaplan, R. S. (1984). "Yesterday's accounting undermines production." *Harvard Business Review*. July/August, and Johnson, H. T., and R. S. Kaplan (1987). *Relevance lost: The rise and fall of management accounting*. Boston: Harvard Business School Press.

13. Kaplan, R. S., and D. P. Norton (2000). *The strategy focused organization: How balanced scorecard companies thrive in the new business environment*. Boston: Harvard Business School Press.

14. Heller, R. (1998). *In search of European excellence: The 10 key strategies of Europe's top companies*. London: HarperCollinsBusiness.

15. Armstrong, M., and A. Baron (1998). *Performance management: The new realities*. London: Institute of Personnel and Development.

16. Institute of Management Accountants (1998). *Tools and techniques for implementing integrated performance management systems*. Statement 4DD, Montvale, NJ: Institute of Management Accountants.

17. Rucci, A. J., S. P. Kirn, and R. T. Quinn (1998). "The employee–customer–profit chain at Sears." *Harvard Business Review*. January/February.

18. Schiemann, W. A., and J. H. Lingle (1999). *Bullseye! Hitting your strategic targets through high-impact measurement*. New York: The Free Press.

19. Gubman, E. L. (1998). *The talent solution: Aligning strategy and people to achieve extraordinary results.* New York: McGraw-Hill.
20. Armstrong and Baron. *Performance management: The new realities.*
21. Berenschot (1999). *Goed performance management loont, onderzoek prestatiemeting bij grote bedrijven* (transl. Good performance management pays off, performance measurement research at large companies). Berenschot Group B.V., Amsterdam, The Netherlands.
22. Chenhall, R. H., and K. Langfield-Smith (1998). "Adoption and benefits of management accounting practices: An Australian study." *Management Accounting Research* 9:1–19.
23. Low, J., and T. Siesfeld (1998). "Measures that matter: Non-financial performance." *Strategy & Leadership* 26, 2.
24. Frigo, M. (2000). "Current trends in performance measurement systems." In A. Neely, ed., *Performance measurement—past, present and future.* Cranfield: Centre for Business Performance, Cranfield University, 153–160.
25. Mavrinac, S., and M. Vitale (1997). "Where are they now? Revisiting the original balanced scorecard firms." *Measuring Business Performance* 2.
26. Kaplan and Norton. *The strategy-focused organization: How balanced scorecard companies thrive in the new business environment.*
27. Holloway, J. A. (2000). "Investigating the impact of performance measurement." In A. Neely, ed., *Performance measurement—past, present and future.* Cranfield, United Kingdom: Centre for Business Performance, Cranfield University, 234–241.
28. Neely, A., ed. (2000). *Performance measurement—past, present and future.* Cranfield, United Kingdom: Centre for Business Performance, Cranfield University.
29. Zairi, M. (1994). *Measuring Performance for Business Results.* Chapman and Hall; Ashton, C. (1997). *Strategic Performance measurement: Transforming corporate performance by measuring and managing the drivers of business success.* Business Intelligence, Lomoon.
30. Hartmann, F. G. H. (2000). "The appropriateness of RAPM: Toward the further development of theory." *Accounting, Organizations and Society* 25:451–482; Vodosek, M., and K. M. Sutcliffe (2000). "Overemphasis on analysis: Decision-making dilemmas in the age of speed." In Quinn, R. E., R. M. O'Neill, and L. St.Clair (eds.), *Pressing problems in modern organizations (that keep us up at night).* New York: AMACOM.
31. Anthony, R. N. (1965). *Planning and control systems: A framework for analysis.* Boston: Harvard University Press.

2

IDENTIFYING THE
BEHAVIORAL FACTORS

In Chapter 1, a brief description was given of the history of performance management systems and an assessment was made of the need to identify behavioral factors that are important to successful design, implementation, and use of a such a system. In this chapter, these behavioral factors are described.

CRITERIA FOR REGULAR USE

Since the objective of this book is to identify which behavioral factors are important to the *successful* implementation and use of a performance management system, criteria for regular use have been formulated. These criteria denote when use of the performance management system and its critical success factors (CSFs), key performance indicators (KPIs), and balanced scorecard (BSC) is valuable to the organization and its managers. The criteria are a mix of tangible and intangible benefits but focus more on the intangibles. It must be noted that a successful implementation and use of a performance management system does not necessarily mean that the organization has its performance management system embedded in the planning and control cycle with periodic reporting and discussion. Successful implementation and use can already be achieved when the managers have an intensified awareness of the importance of the performance management system. The criteria for regular use are given in Exhibit 2.1, in the format of interview questions.

Exhibit 2.1   **Criteria for Regular Use**

1. Are the results of the organization, according to managers, improved through the use of the performance management system?

2. Are the results of the organization, objectively, improved through use of the performance management system?

3. Has the degree of performance management system use by managers increased?

4. Are there plans for follow-up projects?

5. Is there a difference in manager attitude toward performance management, from project start to currently?

6. Is there regular communication about KPI results?

7. Are the CSFs, KPIs, and BSC incorporated in the regular management reporting?

BEHAVIORAL FACTORS

As was stated before, many behavioral factors can contribute to the successful implementation and use of a performance management system. In order to make the investigation into these behavioral factors manageable, they have been grouped and arranged in a so-called classification scheme (Exhibit 2.2).

The classification scheme is developed by linking factors of effective control with the control cycle of performance measurement. The controlled system is a manager, the controlling system is the superior of this manager. Efficient management control is determined by the degree of manageability of the controlled system and the management capacity of the controlling system. The internal environment and the external environment also have influence on the degree of control effectiveness. For effective control, the controlled system and controlling system both need a performance management system. Through the performance management system, the controlling system gets information about the performance of the controlled system, and the controlled system obtains information about its own performance. This system can be subdivided into several parts. The development method part describes the way in which the performance management system is developed. The content part stipulates the quality criteria that the performance management system, and the CSFs, KPIs, and BSC it contains, must meet in order to be relevant to both the controlling and controlled system. The feedback part describes the way in which information from the performance management system is conveyed to both the controlling and controlled system. The classification scheme can be further detailed into subparts (Exhibit 2.3).

Exhibit 2.2   Classification Scheme of Behavioral Factors

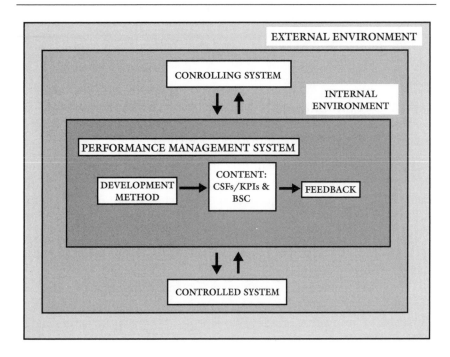

Exhibit 2.3   Subparts of the Classification Scheme

Classification Scheme Part	*Subpart*
Performance management system—Development method	Development method
Performance management system—Content	Quality (criteria for indicators) Registration (of indicators) Purpose (of indicators) Targets (for indicators) Balance (of performance management system)
Performance management system—Feedback	Feed forward (with prognoses) Feedback (through reporting)
Controlled system	Management level Management style
Controlling system	Responsibility Supervision (by promoter) Relationship with controlled system
Internal environment	Alignment (with strategy and business processes) Organizational culture (including structure)
External environment	External environment

In the remainder of this chapter, behavioral factors applicable for each subpart are described. The behavioral factors are derived from the requirements that, according to the literature, have to be taken into account during the development, implementation, and use of a performance management system.

PERFORMANCE MANAGEMENT SYSTEM

Development Method

The performance management system has to be developed in a structured manner. The *development method* constitutes a description of the way in which the performance management system and its CSFs, KPIs, and BSC must be developed and imbedded in the organization. Included in the description are the project approach, assembly of the project team, starting time of the performance management system project, and a change management approach.

The development of the performance management system is not just a technical issue; many change management issues also come into play. Managers often do not (readily) understand the performance management system, do not understand why so much effort should go into "just another system," or are afraid the system makes their performance (too) visible. This can cause resistance, which frustrates the introduction of the system. Investing in the creation of a support base for the performance management system during the development stage is for this reason very important. This can be done by showing the reasons and goals for introducing the performance management system to the managers. These reasons can be: the continuity of the organization is at stake (e.g., due to bad financial results), dissatisfied customers, worse benchmark figures than the competition, current management reporting does not provide enough insight in the execution of the strategy and crucial business processes, or it costs too much effort to generate the current management reporting while managers are discontent with the content of the reports. A performance management system could give insight into these issues and help managers solve them, so the continuity of the organization and of their positions is guaranteed. If managers are convinced by these arguments, they will support the implementation of performance management and the performance management system. The requirements described above are combined into the behavioral factor: *Managers accept the need for performance management.*

Future users of the performance management system can participate during the performance management system development stage in two ways. Active participation entails the identification of CSFs and KPIs by the users themselves, for their own responsibility areas. Passive participation entails the users giving feedback on the CSFs and KPIs identified by a project team. Whatever the manner of participation chosen, users from many organizational disciplines should be involved as early as possible. Involving many disciplines results in a broader acceptance base for the performance management system and in a better coverage of the important business functions by the performance management system. Involving users at an early stage gives them a better possibility to influence the end results. An additional benefit is that users get a clear insight into the mission and strategy of the organization and how they can influence these to obtain a better organizational performance. Involvement in the development of CSFs, KPIs, and the BSC increases the motivation of users to use the performance management system due to their input in the design of the performance management system. An active role also prevents the "not invented here" syndrome, in which users get new things forced on them. The requirements described above are combined into the behavioral factor: *Managers have an active role during the development stage of the performance management system project.*

Choosing the right starting time for the development of a performance management system is crucial for the acceptance of the system. The organization and its managers have to be ready for such a far-reaching project. If the organization does not have a clearly defined mission and strategy, if there are many operational problems, or if there are not enough resources, then it is probably better to wait with the development of the performance management system until a more appropriate starting time. In the organization, there has to be a consensus that the chosen starting time is indeed appropriate. An appropriate starting time is when managers have enough time to spend on the project or when there is a clear, urgent need for better management information. Managers have to be involved in the decision about the starting time, so they have a better insight into the decision-making process and also can guarantee their participation. If there is no consensus or if managers have not been involved in the decision about the starting time, they may resist the project and may not cooperate. The requirements described above are combined into the behavioral factors: *Managers agree on the starting time* and *Managers have been involved in decision making around the project start time.*

Regular and structured communication needs to take place with all persons involved in the development of the performance management system. There should not be only communication about the reasons for the introduction of the performance management system and about intermediary project results, but also about daily project activities. For this, a communication plan is needed, describing the communication moments, content, communication manner (formal or informal), and communication receivers. An integral part of the communication should be a feedback mechanism from the organization to the project team, so a dialogue between the two is set up.

A change in management information and the performance management system can lead to uneasiness and unrest in the organization. For instance, the unexpected confrontation with results on KPIs can cause great resistance by managers. Regular communication increases managers' knowledge about the project (unknown, unloved) and can defuse a potential time bomb under the project. An added benefit of regular communication is that managers get a better insight into the motives to introduce the performance management system. Communication will have a positive influence on the degree of acceptance of the system, which will increase even more when the future users of the performance management system participate themselves in the communication process. The requirements described above are combined into the behavioral factors: *Managers are informed about the status of the performance management system project* and *Managers are actively communicating about the performance management system project.*

Content

The content of the performance management system can originate from several different sources and must meet certain standards. The content has to be of good *quality:* CSFs and KPIs have to be clearly defined, valid, relevant, and measurable. In order to be able to report KPIs, *registration* of relevant data has to take place: Data must be collected, calculated, and stored in the performance management system. The CSFs, KPIs, and the BSC need a clear *purpose,* which is the monitoring of the execution of the strategy, of the performance on critical business activities, and of significant (temporary) developments in the internal and external environments. The CSFs and KPIs must be in *balance,* which means that they monitor all relevant and critical aspects of the business. Finally, all the KPIs need to have *targets,* so that the performance levels the organization strives for are clear.

Quality. KPIs must be defined clearly, which means they need to have an intelligible and consistent definition. A KPI is intelligible for managers if it is defined in terms that they understand and that match their daily practice, and when the indicator is not complex. In this way, the

KPI is understood by the managers who have to work with them. Managers can also better judge the effect their activities have on the KPI result and tailor their activities to get a better result or tailor the KPIs so they better represent their responsibility areas. A KPI definition is consistent if the definition stays the same through time. This is important for making relevant and meaningful comparisons over time. A KPI that is defined in an unclear, vague, or overly technical way causes confusion and misinterpretation. A good way to increase the understanding of managers is to involve them in defining their own KPIs. This will also increase the support for the new indicators. The requirements described above are combined into the behavioral factors: *Managers understand the meaning of KPIs* and *Managers are involved in defining KPIs.*

It is to be expected that the results attained on KPIs will lead directly or indirectly to financial consequences. According to the American Productivity & Quality Center, best practice organizations are able to display relationships among their performance management systems, human asset management results (e.g., retention, development, succession planning) and, to a lesser extent, financially driven business results.[1] In addition, the relationship between nonfinancial indicators and financial results is often unclear and difficult to quantify for managers. In practice, managers often stick to financial indicators that have an explicit and clear relation with the financial result. As a consequence, the softer indicator such as client satisfaction or employee motivation is often left out. These indicators, however, are crucial to the continuity for an organization because they are indicators of future profitability and added value: A bad result on them will eventually lead to a bad financial result. If relationships, however difficult, can be established between nonfinancial indicators, actions taken on these will improve the organization's financial results, and acceptance of these types of KPIs by managers will increase. These relationships will also make more clear to managers what the financial consequences of their activities will be. The requirements described above are combined into the behavioral factor: *Managers have insight into the relationship between KPIs and financial results.*

Registration. The data needed to calculate the results on the KPIs can come from several sources. They can be registered internally, manually, or via internal information systems, or they can come from external sources, like opinion polls and market surveys. Often, there exists a preference in the organization to define KPIs that can be calculated from existing (operational and financial) data sources and information systems because these do not take too much effort to report. In itself, this is not a short-coming as the organization has a lot of valuable information which should not be ignored in the performance management system. However, an organization should not base its information supply solely on operational and financial indicators. Instead, it should also include important nonfinancial indicators that may not be readily available, like client satisfaction and employee satisfaction, in its management reporting. Because at many organizations it takes great effort to generate data for many of the nonfinancial indicators, the result is often new management information that more or less resembles the old information set. Consequently, supplementary procedures and systems are needed to guarantee an automatic supply of nonfinancial indicators. This will save a lot of time and effort of managers in collecting and reporting this type of information, preventing managers from thinking of nonfinancial reporting as an extra workload and decreasing the chance of their resisting the performance management system. The requirements described above are combined into the behavioral factor: *Managers do not get discouraged by the collection of performance data.*

Purpose. The strategy of an organization can be operationalized and made tangible by defining CSFs and KPIs. Because the strategy indicates the long-term goals of the organization, these CSFs and KPIs foster thinking about long-term performance. In addition, by using these CSFs and KPIs, managers are better able to see which results the organization obtains, having a motivational effect. For this to work, there needs to be consensus among managers about the strategy, the strategy must be translated in operational goals that incite action, and there must be a clear linkage between these operational goals, organizational performance, and organizational strategy. The requirements described above are combined into the behavioral factor: *Managers have insight into the relationship between strategy and CSFs/KPIs.*

Besides the strategy, the business processes of an organization can also be the basis for CSFs and KPIs. Because (especially complex) organizations dispose of a great variety of business processes and activities, only the crucial processes and activities should be taken as the basis for the indicators. Crucial processes and activities are defined by them as those that are critical for the continuity of the organization. Measuring these processes with tangible KPIs makes it easier for managers to see how their performance on these activities influence the overall performance of the organization on crucial business processes. The requirements described above are combined into the behavioral factor: *Managers have insight into the relationship between business processes and CSFs/KPIs.*

Balance. The set of defined CSFs and KPIs has to provide a well-balanced overview of the actual performance of an organization. This means that a performance management system must be created that contains not only financial but also nonfinancial indicators; not only quantitative but also qualitative indicators; not only internal but also external indicators; and not only short-term but also long-term indicators. Indicators have only a signaling function. They give an abstract and partial view of reality. It is not possible to provide a complete view with one indicator. Consequently, managers need a balanced set to get an overview of their responsibility area. Such a set makes it possible for managers to explain the results in their responsibility area in a multidimensional way, and to see the cause-and-effect relationship between their activities and their results. The requirements described above are combined into the behavioral factors: *Managers' KPI sets are aligned with their responsibility areas* and *Managers have insight into the relationship between cause and effect.*

Targets. Targets are the performance levels an organization strives for. Managers are involved in the process of target setting if they (the controlled system) have the freedom to negotiate the targets with their superiors (the controlling system). During this negotiation, managers and superiors exchange information about the nature and feasibility of the targets. In addition, managers have the opportunity to influence the expected performance levels. This results in a greater degree of understanding of what is expected and a higher acceptance by managers of the agreed-upon performance levels. Managers are also more motivated to reach the agreed-upon targets, resulting in better overall organizational performance. However, targets should not just be the result of negotiations without taking into account stakeholder requirements, fundamental process limits, and improvement process capabilities. It should be kept in mind that managers, when participating in setting targets, might be tempted to manipulate the process in order to obtain easier targets. The requirements described above are combined into the behavioral factor: *Managers are involved in setting KPI targets.*

Feedback

As soon as an organization starts using the performance management system, information about performance on the CSFs and KPIs must be reported. Managers receive *feedback* information in the format of management information on realized performance. Feedback makes it possible for managers to analyze results and take corrective actions. Managers receive *feed forward* information in the format of prognoses on expected performance. Feed forward makes it possible for managers to make estimations about future results and to take preventative action.

Feed forward. Many performance management systems give only the actuals to date, with limited attention being paid to future expectations by including prognoses in the reports. Too often, management assumes that good results in the past are a guarantee for good results in the future, but they are not. In today's turbulent, dynamic, and quickly changing business environment, future expectations are sorely needed. If managers make prognoses for their responsibility areas, they are not only better prepared on what is to come but they can also undertake preventative action, if needed. These prognoses have to be of a good quality, so that managers have good insight into their areas and future performances. This will increase trust not only in the defined KPIs but also in their own management abilities. The requirements described above are combined into the behavioral factors: *Managers are involved in forecasting* and *Managers trust good quality forecasts.*

The performance management system has to support managers actively in the execution of their activities. Consequently, the performance management system must provide managers with the information that makes it possible for them to undertake corrective and preventative action. The key to a successful organization lies in its willingness to start using and acting on the information provided by the performance management system. The performance management system is action oriented if it contains information for taking action and enables managers to follow the execution of these actions and their results. If this is possible, managers will be greatly motivated because the performance management system helps them to solve issues, prevent problems, and obtain higher performance. The requirements described above are combined into the behavioral factor: *Managers' activities are supported by KPIs.*

Managers need to compare their results with managers of other organizational units or even of other organizations. This means that KPIs have to be comparable throughout the organization: They must have the same meaning, the same definition, and the same method of calculation. KPIs should also fit the frame of reference of managers, so managers can understand the comparisons between their performance and those of others. Making KPIs comparable has as an added advantage in that the organization can put its performance in perspective by benchmarking it against that of other organizations. This helps managers to learn whether their performance is on par or whether it should be improved. Comparing KPIs is, however, not so straightforward. The moment of measuring and comparing KPIs is important. New systems are often implemented when things are not going so well for the organization. The chance of performance improvement anyway is therefore quite good. However, this will distort the result (in a positive way) of the KPI, making it less comparable. For many nonfinancial indicators, there will be a time lag before improvements show up. This has to be taken into account when considering the timing of making the comparison. The requirements described above are combined into the behavioral factor: *Managers' frames of reference contains similar KPIs.*

Feedback.   Management information is intelligible for users if the performance management system is easy to understand. The use of colors, graphs, tables, standard formats, and standard interfaces make the performance management system accessible. The principle should be that "one picture says more than a thousand words." Text supporting graphs should be short and concise. A good method to make an intelligible performance management system is to let the managers participate in the design of the system. This will give managers a greater insight into the structure and setup of the performance management system and will also make sure it is better tailored to their needs. This increases the acceptance of the performance management system. The requirements described above are combined into the behavioral factors: *Managers are involved in making the CSF/KPI/BSC report layout* and *Managers understand the CSF/KPI/ BSC reporting.*

Reliable information consists of data that has been measured systematically and objectively without distortion, interference, or manipulation of managers and that can be verified by independent sources. There is a lot of literature about the positive relationship between reliability of feedback and acceptance of feedback. If the receiver of the feedback considers this feedback to be reliable (i.e., an accurate depiction of his or her performance), then he or she will accept that feedback. This means the receiver will base his or her decisions and course of action on this feedback, which in turn will lead to better performance. The requirements described above are combined into the behavioral factor: *Managers trust the performance information.*

During information analysis, managers look at the deviation between targets (budgeted values) and actuals (realized values). Of interest are magnitude, cause, type, and tendency of the deviation. Type means whether the deviation is incidental (question is then: for how long?) or structural (question is then: what are the future consequences?). The degree to which analyses are made by managers indicates how much the performance management system is used by these managers. The fact that managers make their own analyses will raise the quality of the analyses because these managers know best what is happening in their responsibility areas and are, therefore, in the best position to formulate corrective actions. It will also raise acceptance of the analyses because these are not forced on managers by a relative outsider. A precondition is that the performance management system makes information openly available, so that the manager can trust good quality analyses with enough depth. The requirements described above are combined into the behavioral factors: *Managers are involved in making analyses* and *Managers trust good-quality analyses.*

CONTROLLED SYSTEM

The controlled system uses the performance management system to obtain information about the responsibility area, for self-control and self-management, and for accountability to the controlling system. Every *management level* has its own specific CSF/KPI set and specific BSC. Because there are several management levels in one organization, there will be several sets of indicators and scorecards. There is a specific *management style* that a manager has to apply if he or she uses the performance management system in the communication upward to superior and downward to employees.

Management Level

Because different management levels have different responsibilities, there must be more than one set of CSFs, KPIs, and BSCs in the organization, each representing these different responsibilities. Managers use those indicators that give them the best information for their decision-making process. In this way, every management level receives the information that is relevant to that level. Often, the set for top management will consist of mainly financial and long-term indicators. The lower in the organization the level, the more operational and short-term the indicator set will become. If the CSF/KPI sets are not specific enough, the performance management system is not able to support managers in making their decisions and in obtaining their specific goals because the provided information is not relevant and specific enough. This will lower the acceptance of the performance management system. The requirements described above are combined into the behavioral factor: *Managers use the CSFs/KPIs/BSC that match their responsibility areas.*

A manager can become overloaded with information. Many things can be measured but then the manager has to spend too much time measuring and trying to shift to the obtained data to get to the real valuable information. As Nobel-prize winning economist Herbert Simon put it: "A wealth of information creates a poverty of attention."[2] This overload fragments the manager's attention and effort. To prevent the problem, managers need to receive that amount of information that is needed to represent fairly their responsibility areas. This means, in general, limiting the CSF/KPI set to the critical indicators, 5 to a maximum of 15 indicators per organizational unit. The best way to limit the KPIs is to let managers choose their own because they know best which indicators accurately monitor their activities. After choosing the set, managers should be able to spend enough time on working with these indicators. Because the set is limited, managers will not spend too much time. However, if they do not get enough time due to other work pressures or too many special tasks, they will not get enough added value out of their KPIs. The requirements described above are combined into the behavioral factors: *Managers' information processing capabilities are not exceeded by the number of CSFs/KPIs* and *Managers have enough time to work with their CSFs/KPIs/BSC.*

Management Style

Various management styles can be distinguished like management by numbers, management by walking around, management by objectives, and participative management style. This investigation focuses on the style a manager uses when applying the performance management system in managing subordinates, managing himself or herself, and communicating with superiors. What differentiates today's high-performing companies are the capabilities and behaviors associated with effective information use: the so-called information orientation of the company and its leaders.[3] A positive information orientation or attitude toward the performance management system and performance management entails that managers recognize the value of the new system for supporting their activities like managing employees and in obtaining targets, which fosters the acceptance of the new system. Managers who have previously had positive experiences with CSFs, KPIs, and the BSC often have a positive attitude toward performance management. A positive attitude can be affected negatively when the new system, which makes performance transparent, is going to be used to punish bad results. Managers will then start to resist the performance management system and will manipulate the information in the system. The requirements described above are combined into the behavioral factors: *Managers have earlier (positive) experiences with performance management, Managers realize the impor-*

tance of CSFs/KPIs/BSC to their performance, Managers can use their CSFs/ KPIs/BSC for managing their employees, and Managers do not experience CSFs/KPIs/BSC as threatening.

CONTROLLING SYSTEM

The controlling system is the superior of a manager. Managers use the information from the performance management system for accountability purposes and in this way can report and explain performance to their superior. The way this happens is governed by the planning and control cycle that exists in the organization. This cycle stipulates the *relationship with the controlled system* (the communication that has to take place between manager and superior), using the *specific indicators for which a manager is responsible*. The controlling system must appoint a specific person to sponsor and *supervise* the development, implementation, and use of the performance management system.

Responsibility

For each KPI, a single manager should be appointed who is formally responsible for the results of that indicator. This makes responsibility obvious when an issue arises around a particular indicator. If accountabilities for KPIs are not clear, the indicators can be viewed as being for information only. As a consequence, either the indicator will not be managed, resulting in late action and bad performance, or many discussions will take place between managers. If results are bad, managers may put the blame on each other; if results are good, managers may undeservedly claim the glory. To prevent disagreements at a later date, managers should be involved when appointing indicators to people. Involvement will also raise the acceptance level of the accountability. The requirements described above are combined into the behavioral factors: *Managers have sole responsibility for a KPI* and *Managers can influence the KPIs assigned to them.*

Supervision

During the development and implementation of the performance management system, a sponsor from top management should be appointed who has to supervise the project and who is responsible for a successful implementation. This person has to be acceptable to the organization based on experience, seniority, or other criteria. If the sponsor is not accepted by the organization, the individual will not be able to influence the project activities enough to make sure the project can be finalized successfully. If the sponsor has been accepted, the sponsor must make sure to spend enough time on the project. Then, the organization will see the promoter takes the project seriously. Because the implementation of a performance management system takes a lot of the organization's effort. Active and visible support of the project by top management is essential to convey the importance of the new system to the organization. Top management (the controlling system) has to use the performance management system frequently and visibly in dealings with the controlled systems and must regularly communicate the results from the performance management system to the organization. For instance, this can be done by regularly scheduling meetings to discuss the performance management system results. The requirements described above are combined into the behavioral factors: *Managers accept the promoter, Managers see the promoter spends enough time on the performance management system implementation,* and *Managers clearly see the promoter using the performance management system.*

Relationship with Controlled System

In the relationship between controlling system and controlled system, there has to be a certain degree of trust in order to be able to use the performance management system effectively. This is because the performance management system makes the performance of the controlled system much more transparent than the traditional financial-based reporting system did. This makes the controlled system more vulnerable to criticism from the controlling system. If the controlling system then uses the information to punish or sanction the controlled system, the latter will not trust that the former makes appropriate use of the system. Managers will start to resent the performance management system and will sabotage it. The requirements described above are combined into the behavioral factor: *Managers and their controlling systems have a mutual trust.*

INTERNAL ENVIRONMENT

The internal environment constitutes the inside world or the context in which the performance management system, the controlled system, and the controlling system exist and operate. Since development and adjustment of the strategy, the business processes, and the planning and control cycle take place continuously, an organization has to make sure there is *alignment* between strategy, processes, and the performance management system. This means the performance management system, CSFs, KPIs, and BSC need to be updated regularly to reflect the new situation of the organization. Effective use of the performance management system requires a change in *organizational culture:* from a focus on punishment to a focus on improvement. This must be reflected in the reward structure and communication processes of the organization.

Alignment

Rapid changes in the market (e.g., competitors' actions, recessions) and inside the organization (e.g., reorganization, personnel turnover) force the organization to adapt its strategy and business processes constantly. This, in turn, causes adaptation of the performance management system, CSFs, KPIs, and the BSC, which are monitoring the strategy and processes. Consequently, an organization has to review and update its performance management system regularly to make sure it still accurately represents the organization's performance. According to the American Productivity & Quality Center, best-practice organizations recognize the need to monitor continuously and improve the performance management process.[4] This review and adaptation of the performance management system can take place during the annual planning process, making it an integral part of the organization's planning and control cycle. During the update, consensus needs to exist among the managers about the changes to be made in the performance management system so these changes will be accepted by them. If review and adaptation do not take place, the quality of the information from the performance management system will decrease, thereby losing its relevance to the managers, who will be inclined to use the system less and less. The requirements described above are combined into the behavioral factors: *Managers find the performance management system relevant due to regular evaluations, Managers use the performance management system regularly during the planning and control cycle,* and *Managers agree on changes in the CSF/KPI set.*

Organizational Culture

Regular and frequent use of the performance management system requires alignment between the culture of the organization and the culture that is needed to practice performance management. This culture needs to be based on performance improvement, self-control, and learning—not on punishment. This improvement culture, in which mistakes are seen as sources for improvement and not as causes for punishment, can be characterized as a culture in which there exists a small distance between controlling system and controlled system, collectivism, absence of masculine role patterns, long-term orientation, and a great degree of tolerance for ambiguity.[5] This culture stimulates managers to use the results of their KPIs as the starting point for improvement actions. If an organization uses the performance management system solely for accountability and punishment purposes, there will be a great incentive for managers to start manipulating the figures and optimizing the KPI results without necessarily solving underlying problems. The requirements described above are combined into the behavioral factor: *Managers are stimulated to improve their performance.*

In an organization, there can exist a (relatively) tranquil and stable or a turbulent working environment. In case of the latter, managers are confronted with many conflicts, overtime, unfinished business, and stress. In a stable environment, these kind of situations occur considerably less frequently. The working environment can impact the implementation of a performance management system dramatically. In a turbulent situation, managers will not have enough time, attention span, or energy to spend on the implementation of and learning the performance management system. The requirements described above are combined into the behavioral factor: *Managers work in a stable, relatively tranquil environment.*

An open communication structure is important to convey the reasons for the performance management system and the status of the performance management system implementation. The results of the CSFs, KPIs, and BSC must be freely available to everybody in the organization. In this way, people in the organization are informed about their own results and the result of the overall organization. This will increase trust in each other and in the system. An added benefit is that openness makes comparisons between organizational units easier (benchmarking). If there is inadequate openness, distrust and fear for the performance management system will start to appear, especially if people think the system will be used for punishment. The requirements described above are combined into the behavioral factor: *Managers' results on CSFs/KPIs/BSC are openly communicated.*

There is a strong body of opinion in both psychology and accounting, which suggests that performance measures are likely to have a stronger impact on individuals' reactions and on their subsequent behavior if the indicators are used to evaluate the individuals' performance. Thus, it seems likely that members of organizations will be encouraged to react more responsively to feedback from performance measures if they are evaluated on the measures. For this reason, the implementation of a performance management system has to be supported by the reward system of the organization. It is important that the reward system positively reinforces desired behavior. Consequently, the performance management system and the reward system must be aligned, so managers are adequately rewarded for the desired results on their KPIs. Rewards function as incentive for managers to use the performance management system. The requirements described above are combined into the behavioral factor: *Managers' use of the performance management system is stimulated by the reward structure.*

EXTERNAL ENVIRONMENT

The *external environment* comprises the outside world or the context in which the organization (the internal environment) exists and operates. The performance management system must be able to monitor significant developments in the industry and the macroenvironment in which the organization operates.

Organizations have to deal with several external stakeholders, like banks, stockholders, supervisory board, and unions. All these parties request information from the organization for their own purposes. Consequently, they would like to influence the content of the organization's performance management system. The organization has to provide this information to a certain degree. By incorporating crucial stakeholders' information needs in the performance management system, the organization becomes more responsive to the outside world and competitors. This advantage must be weighed against the risk of tailoring the performance management system too much to the requirements of the outside world so that the information of the performance management system does not adequately cover the responsibility areas of the managers anymore. The requirements described above are combined into the behavioral factor: *Managers find the performance management system relevant because only those stakeholders' interests are incorporated that are important to the organization's success.*

The requirements that the law puts on external reporting can severely influence content and structure of periodic reporting. Incorporating crucial external reporting requirements in the performance management system makes the organization more responsive to the outside world. However, these outside information demands can be so strong that the internal reporting loses its relevance for managers. The figures and calculations can be set up in a way to satisfy external demands, but in this way they can lose the meaning for internal control purposes. If this happens, there is a chance the information of the performance management system does not adequately cover the responsibility areas of managers anymore, decreasing their faith in the performance management system. Research shows that external reporting requirements have an indirect influence on reporting by management teams. Consequences of certain organizational decisions, which could show up unfavorably in the external reporting, were managed in such a way by managers that the internal reporting was changed so that favorable external reporting could be derived from it. This made the internal reports less (directly) relevant for managers. The requirements described above are combined into the behavioral factor: *Managers find the performance management system relevant because it has a clear internal control purpose.*

OVERVIEW OF BEHAVIORAL FACTORS

Exhibit 2.4 contains the selected behavioral factors, per subpart of the classification scheme. For each behavioral factor, a clarification question is given to illuminate the meaning of the factor.

Exhibit 2.4 **Listing of the Behavioral Factors per Classification Scheme Part and Subpart**

Classification Scheme Part	Subpart	Behavioral Factor	Clarification Question
Performance management system— Development method	Development method	Managers accept the need for performance management.	Has the need for performance measurement been demonstrated?
		Managers have an active role during the development stage of the performance management system project.	Are users sufficiently involved during development stage?
		Managers agree on the starting time.	Has the appropriate starting time for performance management system project been chosen?

(continues)

Exhibit 2.4 **Continued**

Classification Scheme Part	Subpart	Behavioral Factor	Clarification Question
Performance management system— Development method *(continued)*	Development method *(continued)*	Managers have been involved in decision making about the project start time.	
		Managers are informed about the status of the performance management system project.	Does regular communication take place during the project?
		Managers are actively communicating about the performance management system project.	
Performance management system— Content	Quality	Managers understand the meaning of KPIs.	Have KPIs been clearly defined?
		Managers are involved in defining KPIs.	
		Managers have insight into the relationship between KPIs and financial results.	Is the relationship between KPIs and financial results sufficiently clear?
	Registration	Managers do not get discouraged by the collection of performance data.	Is performance data collected with information systems?
	Purpose	Managers have insight into the relationship between strategy and CSFs/KPIs.	Is the relationship between strategy and CSFs/KPIs sufficiently clear?
		Managers have insight into the relationship between business processes and CSFs/KPIs.	Is the relationship between business processes and CSFs/KPIs sufficiently clear?
	Targets	Managers are involved in setting KPI targets.	Are users sufficiently involved during target setting?

Exhibit 2.4 **Continued**

Classification Scheme Part	Subpart	Behavioral Factor	Clarification Question
Performance management system— Content (continued)	Balance	Managers' KPI sets are aligned with their responsibility areas.	Has a balanced set of KPIs been made?
		Managers have insight into the relationship between cause and effect.	
Performance management system— Feedback	Feed forward	Managers are involved in forecasting.	Is the performance management system sufficiently future oriented?
		Managers trust good-quality forecasts.	
		Managers' activities are supported by KPIs.	Is the performance management system sufficiently action oriented?
		Managers' frames of reference contain similar KPIs.	Are KPIs mutually comparable?
	Feedback	Managers are involved in making the CSF/KPI/BSC report layout.	Is the performance management system sufficiently intelligible?
		Managers understand the CSF/KPI/BSC reporting.	
		Managers trust the performance information.	Is the information in the performance management system reliable?
		Managers are involved in making analyses.	Has the information been sufficiently analyzed?
		Managers trust good-quality analyses.	
Controlled system	Management level	Managers use the CSFs/KPIs/BSC that match their responsibility areas.	Have specific sets of CSFs and KPIs been made for each management level?

(continues)

Exhibit 2.4 **Continued**

Classification Scheme Part	Subpart	Behavioral Factor	Clarification Question
Controlled system (continued)	Management level (continued)	Managers' information processing capabilities are not exceeded by the number of CSFs/KPIs.	Is the number of KPIs per manager limited?
		Managers have enough time to work with their CSFs/KPIs/BSC.	
	Management style	Managers have earlier (positive) experiences with performance management.	Have managers' attitudes toward performance management been checked?
		Managers realize the importance of CSFs/KPIs/BSC to their performance.	
		Managers do not experience CSFs/KPIs/BSC as threatening.	
		Managers can use their CSFs/KPIs/BSC for managing their employees.	
Controlling system	Responsibility	Managers can influence the KPIs assigned to them.	Have managers been made responsible for specific KPIs?
		Managers have sole responsibility for a KPI.	
	Supervision	Managers accept the promoter.	Has a promoter been appointed for the project?
		Managers see that the promoter spends enough time on the performance management system implementation.	

Exhibit 2.4 **Continued**

Classification Scheme Part	Subpart	Behavioral Factor	Clarification Question
Controlling system *(continued)*	Supervision *(continued)*	Managers clearly see the promoter using the performance management system.	
	Relationship with controlled system	Managers and their controlling systems have a mutual trust.	Has the relationship between controlled and controlling systems a positive influence on their working together?
Internal environment	Alignment	Managers find the performance management system relevant due to regular evaluations.	Is the performance management system an integral part of the planning and control cycle?
		Managers use the performance management system regularly during the planning and control cycle.	
		Managers agree on changes in the CSF/KPI set.	
	Organizational culture	Managers are stimulated to improve their performance.	Has a culture of improvement been established?
		Managers work in a stable, relatively tranquil environment.	Has the work situation in the organization been improved?
		Managers' results on CSFs/KPIs/BSC are openly communicated.	Has an open communication structure been established?
		Managers' use of the performance management system is stimulated by the reward structure.	Has the reward structure been aligned with the performance management system?

(continues)

Exhibit 2.4 **Continued**

Classification Scheme Part	Subpart	Behavioral Factor	Clarification Question
External environment	External environment	Managers find the performance management system relevant because only those stakeholders' interests are incorporated that are important to the organization's success.	Has the influence of external stakeholders been limited?
		Managers find the performance management system relevant because it has a clear internal control purpose.	Has the influence of external reporting requirements been limited?

OPERATIONALIZING THE BEHAVIORAL FACTORS

In order to answer the question which seeks to identify which of the behavioral factors (listed in Exhibit 2.4) contribute to successful implementation and use of a performance management system, the identified factors have to be operationalized. This is realized by converting the factors into questions.

The behavioral factors and corresponding questions can be grouped in three stages:

1. The information plan stage, in which the decision to implement a performance management system is taken and a suitable development method is chosen;
2. The measure plan stage, in which the CSFs, KPIs, and the BSC are developed; and
3. The action plan stage, in which the performance management system is put into use.[6]

These stages more or less match the three parts of the performance management system as described in the classification scheme (Exhibit 2.2): development method, content, and feedback. Kaplan and Norton distinguish four stages for developing a performance measurement system: (1) define the measurement architecture (including the choice of the unit where to implement the BSC); (2) build consensus around strategic objectives; (3) select and design measures; and (4) build the implementation plan (including implementing the BSC).[7] If the first two stages of Kaplan and Norton are taken together and their combination is seen as the starting stage, one again arrives at three stages. They are referred to as:

1. Starting stage (S), in which the decision to implement a performance management system is taken;
2. Development stage (D), in which the performance management system is developed; and
3. Use stage (U), in which the performance management system is implemented and put into use.

The behavioral factors, operational questions,[8] and stages are given in Exhibit 2.5.

In Appendix A, an activity plan for conducting a case study is given. Also, the interview list, document research question list, questionnaire, and feedback reporting list of topics that were used during the case studies is

Exhibit 2.5   Behavioral Factors—Operationalized in Interview Questions

Classification Scheme Part	Behavioral Factor	Questions	Influence on Stage
Performance management system— Development method	Managers accept the need for performance management.	■ What were, according to you, the reasons for implementing a performance management system? ■ Do you think that the use of the performance management system is important for the continuity of the organization? If yes, why? If no, why not?	S(1)
	Managers have an active role during the development stage of the performance management system project.	■ How would you describe your role during the implementation of the performance management system: active or reviewing? ■ Were you sufficiently involved during the development of the performance management system, CSFs, and KPIs?	D(1)

(continues)

Exhibit 2.5 **Continued**

Classification Scheme Part	Behavioral Factor	Questions	Influence on Stage
Performance management system— Development method *(continued)*	Managers agree on the starting time.	■ Was, according to you, the right starting time chosen for the implementation? If yes, why? If no, why not?	S(2)
	Managers have been involved in decision making about the project start time.	■ Were you involved in the decision making about the project start time? If yes, how?	S(3)
	Managers are informed about the status of the performance management system project.	■ How often were you informed, during the project, about the status of the project? Did you value this communication? Why? ■ Which communication tools were used?	D(2)
	Managers are actively communicating about the performance management system project.	■ How often did you contribute to the communication about the project? ■ Was, during the communication, feedback asked for? ■ Was there any follow up on given feedback?	D(3)
Performance management system— Content	Managers understand the meaning of KPIs.	■ Are you familiar with the definitions of the KPIs? How are these available? ■ How often (per month/year) are these definitions changed?	D(4)
	Managers are involved in defining KPIs.	■ Were you (actively) involved in defining the KPIs?	D(5)
	Managers have insight into the relationship between KPIs and financial results.	■ Do you discern a relationship between the results on KPIs, actions taken, and the organization's financial results? ■ If yes, is this relationship quantified, and how is this done? If no, why not? ■ Are financial consequences of KPI results mentioned in the performance management system?	U(1)

Exhibit 2.5   **Continued**

Classification Scheme Part	Behavioral Factor	Questions	Influence on Stage
Performance management system— Content *(continued)*	Managers do not get discouraged by the collection of performance data.	■ Is the time you and your subordinates spend on collecting data for KPI reporting acceptable? ■ How much of the total data are manually provided?	U(2)
	Managers have insight into the relationship between strategy and CSFs/KPIs.	■ Does the current CSF/KPI set measure the strategic goals of the organization adequately? If yes, which goals are being measured? If no, why not?	D(6)
	Managers have insight into the relationship between business processes and CSFs/KPIs.	■ Is there an unambiguous relationship between the CSF /KPI set and the crucial business activities of the organization? If yes, which crucial activities are being measured? If no, why not?	D(7)
	Managers are involved in setting KPI targets.	■ Were you sufficiently involved during the setting of targets for the KPIs? ■ To which degree are KPI targets mentioned in the performance management system?	D(8)
	Managers' KPI sets are aligned with their responsibility areas.	■ Is the current CSF/KPI set an adequate reflection of your responsibility area?	D(9)
	Managers have insight into the relationship between cause and effect.	■ Are there, in your opinion, clear cause-and-effect relationships identified for the KPIs? If yes, how many relationships? If no, why not?	U(3)
Performance management system— Feedback	Managers are involved in forecasting.	■ Are you sufficiently involved in forecasting? How are you involved? ■ How often (per year) are forecasts made?	U(4)

(continues)

Exhibit 2.5   **Continued**

Classification Scheme Part	Behavioral Factor	Questions	Influence on Stage
Performance management system— Feedback *(continued)*	Managers trust good quality forecasts.	■ Has, in your opinion, the quality of the forecasts been improved, compared to the actuals?	U(5)
	Managers' activities are supported by KPIs.	■ To which degree do you undertake actions based on the KPI results? Can you give an example of an action? If you do not take action based on the KPI results, why not? ■ Are these actions better focused and more effective than in the past?	U(6)
	Managers' frames of reference contain similar KPIs.	■ Do you use the CSF/KPI set for comparing your performance with those of other units or organizations? If yes, what are the benefits? If no, why not? ■ Is comparison of results/ benchmarking viewed as threatening in your unit? If yes, why?	U(7)
	Managers are involved in making the CSF/KPI/BSC report layout.	■ Were you sufficiently involved in the reporting layout and content definition?	D(10)
	Managers understand the CSF/KPI/BSC reporting.	■ Are colors, tables, graphs, and standard formats used in the performance management system? ■ How intelligible do you find the performance management system (including volume of reports)?	D(11)
	Managers trust the performance information.	■ How reliable is the performance management system information, in your opinion?	U(8)

Exhibit 2.5 **Continued**

Classification Scheme Part	Behavioral Factor	Questions	Influence on Stage
Performance management system— Feedback *(continued)*	Managers trust the performance information. *(continued)*	■ How often do you have discussions about the reliability of the performance management system?	
	Managers are involved in making analyses.	■ Do you regularly make analyses of the KPI results? How? ■ Are you sufficiently involved in analysis making?	U(9)
	Managers trust good quality analyses.	■ How open are you in your analyses? How serious are your conversations about your analyses? ■ How is in general, in your opinion, the quality of analyses in the organization?	U(10)
Controlled system	Managers use the CSFs/KPIs/BSC that match their responsibility areas.	■ Is the CSF/KPI set a good representation of all the important issues on your management level? ■ Is there a separate, specific CSF/KPI set for each management level?	D(12)
	Managers' information processing capabilities are not exceeded by the number of CSFs/KPIs.	■ Were you sufficiently involved in the priority setting of the KPIs?	U(11)
	Managers have enough time to work with their CSFs/KPIs/BSC.	■ How much time do you spend on working with the performance management system? Is this enough?	U(12)
	Managers have earlier (positive) experiences with performance management.	■ Did you have prior experience with performance management? Was this a positive or a negative experience? ■ Did this experience affect your attitude toward this project?	S(4)

(continues)

Exhibit 2.5 **Continued**

Classification Scheme Part	Behavioral Factor	Questions	Influence on Stage
Controlled system *(continued)*	Managers realize the importance of CSFs/KPIs/BSC to their performance.	▪ Do you find the use of the performance management system, CSFs, and KPIs useful for your role as manager? If yes, why? If no, why not?	U(13)
	Managers do not experience CSFs/KPIs/BSC as threatening.	▪ Are the CSFs/KPIs/BSC threatening to you? Why?	U(14)
	Managers can use their CSFs/KPIs/BSC for managing their employees.	▪ Are there advantages and disadvantages in using performance management when managing subordinates and communicating with superiors? If yes, which? If no, why not?	U(15)
Controlling system	Managers can influence the KPIs assigned to them.	▪ Do you accept responsibility for the CSFs and KPIs appointed to you? ▪ Are you tackled on your performance? ▪ Do you tackle your subordinates on their performance?	D(13)
	Managers have sole responsibility for a KPI.	▪ Are responsible persons appointed for each KPI? ▪ Is per KPI only one person responsible? ▪ Are there KPIs for which there is more than one person responsible? If yes, how are conflicts about these KPIs resolved?	U(16)
	Managers accept the promoter.	▪ Who was the initiator of the performance management system development project? ▪ Who was the promoter of the performance management system development project? ▪ What was the management level of the promoter? ▪ How do you judge the role of the promoter during the project?	D(14)

Exhibit 2.5 **Continued**

Classification Scheme Part	Behavioral Factor	Questions	Influence on Stage
Controlling system *(continued)*	Managers see that the promoter spends enough time on the performance management system implementation.	■ How much time (in hours and as a percentage of his/her time) did the promoter spend on the project?	D(15)
	Managers clearly see the promoter using the performance management system.	■ Does the management team work with the performance management system? ■ How visible is this in the organization?	U(17)
	Managers and their controlling systems have a mutual trust.	■ How do you manage your subordinates: with tight or loose control? ■ How are you managed by your superior: centralized or decentralized? ■ Is there trust between you and your subordinates/superior? ■ How long have you worked with your subordinates/superior? ■ Has this made the implementation of performance management easier?	U(18)
Internal environment	Managers find the performance management system relevant due to regular evaluations.	■ How many times per year is the CSF/KPI set reviewed and evaluated?	U(19)
	Managers use the performance management system regularly during the planning and control cycle.	■ Are CSFs, KPIs, and the BSC part of the yearly planning cycle?	U(20)

(continues)

Exhibit 2.5   **Continued**

Classification Scheme Part	Behavioral Factor	Questions	Influence on Stage
Internal environment *(continued)*	Managers agree on changes in the CSF/KPI set.	■ How many changes are made each time to the CSF/KPI set? ■ Who decides these changes? ■ Have you made suggestions for changes in the CSF/KPI set and have these suggestions been implemented?	U(21)
	Managers are stimulated to improve their performance.	■ How do you characterize the culture of your organization: focused on improvement or on punishment? How does this show?	U(22)
	Managers work in a stable, relatively tranquil environment.	■ Can you, in the light of all your activities, spend enough time on working with the performance management system and your specific KPIs? ■ Do conflicts take place about KPI results? ■ How do you characterize the working environment in your organization: stable or turbulent?	S(5)
	Managers' results on CSFs/KPIs/ BSC are openly communicated.	■ Are the results of all the KPIs reported to all the managers, or does distribution take place per responsibility area? ■ Do performance comparisons take place between managers (ranking)?	U(23)
	Managers' use of the performance management system is stimulated by the reward structure.	■ Are KPI results linked to your reward? If yes, are you happy with this link? If no, why not? ■ Is the reward strictly financial or also nonfinancial? What type of nonfinancial rewards are used?	U(24)
External environment	Managers find the performance management system relevant	■ Who are the external stake-holders? To which degree do they have an influence on the content of the CSF/KPI set?	D(16)

Exhibit 2.5 **Continued**

Classification Scheme Part	Behavioral Factor	Questions	Influence on Stage
External environment *(continued)*	because only those stakeholders' interests are incorporated that are important to the organization's success.	■ How often do conflicts take place with the stakeholders about this set?	
	Managers find the performance management system relevant because it has a clear internal control purpose.	■ Is the CSF/KPI set used for external reporting? ■ Is a separate external reporting set of internal reports being used? ■ What, in your opinion, was the focus during the development of the CSFs and KPIs: external or internal?	D(17)

given. It was guaranteed that questions that could be checked by means of more than one information source indeed appeared more than once.

Importance of Specific Stages

In order for an implementation of a performance management system to be successful, a good and proven development method needs to be applied. In addition to this, the time of starting the performance management system implementation has to be chosen carefully to ensure that there is sufficient time to develop the system. The main performance management system characteristics can be grouped according to a qualitative and rough evaluation of probable contribution of the characteristics to the design and development (similar to the S and D stages in Exhibit 2.5) and use (similar to the U stage in Exhibit 2.5) stages of a performance management system (Exhibit 2.6).

From Exhibit 2.6 it can be concluded that the design and development stage has a better chance than the use stage of including certain characteristics into a performance management system. This gives the basis for a second question to be investigated: *Are behavioral factors from the starting and development stages more important to the successful implementation and use of a performance management system than those of the use stage?*

Exhibit 2.6   **Probable Contribution of Design and Development Stage, and Use of Data Stage to Certain Performance Management System Characteristics**

Characteristic of the Performance Management System	Probable Contribution to:	
	Design & Development	*Use of Data*
Congruent with competitive strategy	High	Low
Composed of financial and nonfinancial performance measures	High	Low
Provide direction and support to continuous improvement activities	High	High
Provide support to identify tendencies and progress in performance	Low	High
Facilitate understanding of cause-and-effect relationships regarding performance	High	High
Intelligible to majority of employees	Medium	High
Cover all company's business processes	High	Low
Real time information about performance	High	High
Dynamic	High	Medium
Induce employees' attitudes	Medium	High
Evaluate group performance instead of individual performance	Medium	High
Allow performance to be compared against competitive benchmarks	High	High
Composed by efficiency and effectiveness performance measures	High	Low
Linked to business processes	High	Low
Be part of individual and organizational learning	Low	High
Composed of integrated process and result performance measures	High	Low
Integrated to management systems	High	High
Provide a perspective of past, present, and future performance	Medium	High

Source: Martins, R. A. (2000). "Use of performance measurement systems: Some thoughts towards a comprehensive approach." In: A. Neely, ed., *Performance measurement—past, present and future*. Cranfield: Centre for Business Performance, Cranfield University, 363–370.

ENDNOTES

1. American Productivity & Quality Center (1999). *Performance management: Tapping your organization's people potential.* APQC Report.
2. As quoted in: Shapiro, C., and H. R. Varian (1999). *Information rules: A strategic guide to the network economy.* Boston: Harvard Business School Press.
3. Marchand, D. A., T. H. Davenport, and T. Dickson (eds.) (2000). *Mastering information management: Complete MBA companion in information management.* Harlow: Prentice Hall Financial Times.
4. American Productivity & Quality Center, *Performance management: Tapping your organization's people potential.*
5. Hofstede, G. (1984). *Culture's consequences: International differences in work-related values.* Newbury Park, CA: Sage.
6. Kerklaan, L. A. F. M., J. Kingman, and F. P. J. van Kleef (1994). *De cockpit van de organisatie* (transl. The cockpit of the organization). Deventer: Kluwer Bedrijfswetenschappen.
7. See the appendix in Kaplan, R. S., and D. P. Norton (1996). *The balanced scorecard: Translating strategy into action.* Boston: Harvard Business School Press.
8. The questions were distributed over the three sources of information collection that were used during the case studies: a questionnaire, an interview protocol, and a document research list.

ENDNOTES

1.

2.

3.

4.

5.

6.

7.

8.

3

CASES

Chapter 2 provided a description of the behavioral factors and criteria for regular use that were operationalized into questions. This chapter describes how the importance of these behavioral factors for the implementation and use of a performance management system is investigated by means of case studies.

DESCRIPTION OF THE CASE STUDIES

The case study organizations consisted of profit and nonprofit organizations in the Netherlands. A prerequisite for being a case was that the participating organization should have had the performance management system at their disposal for at least one to two years at the time of this study. The reason for using this time limit is twofold. On the one hand, the performance management system implementation should be relatively fresh in the minds of the interviewees so questions about the starting and development stages could be answered. On the other hand, the organization should have had sufficient practical experience with the performance management system so questions about the use stage could be answered. If the implementation happened too long ago, distortion may occur because managers have to rely on their memory. As a consequence, their opinion about the performance management system can become distorted.

The following organizations were chosen: Academic Hospital Utrecht, Kadaster (land registry office), and European IT Services (procurement and financial departments of information technology [IT] procurement organization).[1] At each case study organization, the board of management appointed a contact person who was responsible for scheduling interviews and having discussions with and reading the case description. Most of the time, the contact person was either the sponsor of the performance management system or somebody who had been closely involved in its implementation.

The fieldwork was performed in a time span of four weeks to make sure the acquired data from the interviews was based on the same organizational situation and to be able to give timely feedback to the contact person and the organization. Data was acquired in three ways: through an anonymous questionnaire, interviews, and document research. The questionnaire was distributed to a majority of the managers who had the performance management system at their disposal. The questionnaire focused on the purposes the managers used the performance management system for and their attitude toward the performance management system. Interviews of one to two hours each were held with the contact person, the sponsor of the performance management system, the project manager of the performance management system implementation, 5 to 10 users of the performance management system, and the person responsible for the performance management system reporting. Document research took place using a structured review list of the management reports, the information system (if present), user manuals and process descriptions of the reporting process, project documentation, and minutes of management team meetings about the performance management system. Interview writeups were made of all interviews, which were sent back to the interviewees so they could be checked.

After approval on all feedback had been received, the gathered information was integrated in a case study description. The case study description contained a table of the behavioral factors and denoted whether the case study organization satisfied a particular behavioral factor. Scores were awarded using the following score scheme:

    + = The behavioral factor is satisfied
    0 = The behavioral factor is partially satisfied
    − = The behavioral factor is not satisfied
    NA = Insufficient basis to draw a conclusion whether the behavioral
         factor is satisfied or not

Basically, if the results for a particular behavioral factor from the interviews, document research, and questionnaire were all positive, a plus (+) was awarded; if the results were all negative, a minus (−) was given. If the results were either all 0 or not clearly in one direction (e.g., + 0 0, or + − 0), a zero (0) was given. A final score for each stage (S, D, and U) was determined by calculating the average of all behavioral factors grouped under that stage. This was done by awarding each + with 1 point, each 0 with zero points, and each − with −1 point, adding these all up and dividing them by the total number of behavioral factors of that stage. If the average was below − 0.2, the end result was denoted as being −; for an average above + 0.2, the end result was +; and for an average between − 0.2 and + 0.2, the end result was 0.

The case study description also contained an evaluation of whether the criteria for regular use were satisfied, again by combining and discussing all the information gathered. A final score was calculated by taking the average of all criteria scores. The following score scheme was used:

+ = The criterion was clearly improved by the performance management system use

0 = It was unclear whether the criterion was improved by the performance management system use

− = The criterion was clearly not improved by the performance management system use

The scores for the human elements and criteria for regular use are given in the case study descriptions in the next sections.

After all the case study descriptions were finalized and approved, the final analysis took place. The results from the case studies were collected and compared with each other. The results from the final analysis were used to answer the questions described in Chapter 2.

ACADEMIC HOSPITAL UTRECHT

The Academic Hospital Utrecht (in Dutch: Academisch Ziekenhuis Utrecht, abbreviated as AZU) is part of the health care sector in the Netherlands. The Dutch health care sector has undergone many changes in recent years, caused by increasing competition from private clinics, the separation of care into three categories (high-, medium-, and low-complex care—each with its own manner of processing), increased use of technology, need for cost control, and increased attention to quality and client (patient) needs. AZU's goal is to anticipate and react to these changes and become one of the largest and most prominent hospitals in the Netherlands.

The reason to perform case study research at AZU was threefold. First, AZU, at the time of the case study, had worked with a performance management system for over a year. Second, this performance management system was supported by an information technology tool called AZU-score, which was reported to be an example of a system working well. Finally, there were at least 150 users of AZU-score, which made the research population fairly large.

Description of AZU

The organizational structure of AZU is built around specialties, which form the divisions (Exhibit 3.1). The medical centers provide medical support services for the specialties. The operational services provide general operating supporting services. The board of directors is responsible for managing the divisions, centers, and facilities, and it is accountable to the board of supervisors. This organizational structure is highly decentralized because, as is customary in hospitals, the heart of the organization lies in the medical divisions.

Exhibit 3.1 **Simplified Organizational Structure of AZU**

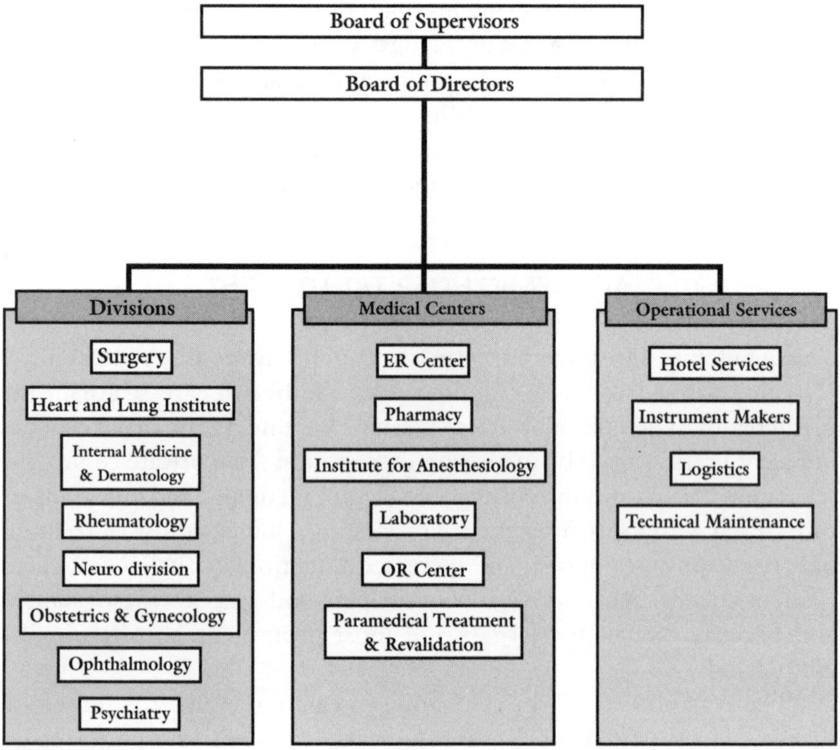

AZU had been steadily growing, both financially and in workforce (Exhibit 3.2). Margins had grown more than turnover through tight cost control and a greater focus on results.

AZU, being a teaching hospital, had formulated an ambitious strategy together with the medical department of the University of Utrecht:

- Provide high-quality patient care and service against reasonable costs, no matter the type or complexity of the patient. AZU should be able to compete in these areas with other large hospitals, focusing on the functions of "top referral" (treating patients who need special expertise) and "last resort" (giving care that patients cannot receive elsewhere in the country).
- Provide for the continuity of this high-quality care by providing training and education to future generations of medical personnel, doctors, and specialists.
- Contribute on an expert level to the international advancement of the medical field in carefully selected areas. The goal of this contribution is to better treat current and future patients.

The changes in the Dutch health care sector, the growth of the hospital, and the ambitions of the organization forced AZU to upgrade its management control and information function. A performance management system was needed to better support the organization; it was decided to undertake the AZU-score project. The goal of the project was to increase the quality of the management control and information function in such a way that the execution of the strategic and divisional plans could be monitored with objective, reliable, timely, and consistent information. Additionally, this information was supposed to make adjustments to the

Exhibit 3.2 **AZU Key Indicators**[a]

Key Indicator	1994	1995
Turnover (x NLG. 1000)	468.881	495.200
Margin (x NLG. 1000)	1.027	3.402
Total personnel (Full-Time Equivalents)	3.926	4.114
FTEs, medical and scientific	194	211
FTEs, medical assistants	205	218
FTEs, nonscientific	2.907	2.985
FTEs, other	621	700

[a] Results over 1996 were not available at the time of the case study.

plans possible, if necessary. The project was executed from September 1995 until October 1996, in three phases:

- *Phase 1: Evaluation.* The board of directors identified 19 key performance indicators (KPIs), which were intended to be used for the communication between the board and managers from the divisions, medical centers, and operational services. These indicators were checked by the AZU-score project team on various quality criteria: simplicity, reliability, timeliness, regular updates, relevancy, and completeness. The evaluation also checked to determine if the indicator could be influenced by the divisional manager. Thirteen KPIs satisfied the quality criteria more or less, and it was decided to roll these out within the organization.
- *Phase 2: Design and implementation.* For each of the 13 indicators, a work group was established. Each work group was responsible for making a concise definition for the KPI, tracking down the manner of data collection, registration, and calculation for the indicator, and checking the results with the organization (Exhibit 3.3). The work group also oversaw the programming of software, needed for the calculation of the KPI in the newly installed AZU-score IT system.

After all the work groups had finalized, the 13 indicators were implemented in four categories: (1) patient mix (three indicators), (2) cost control (four indicators), and (3) service (six indicators). There were no indicators identified for the fourth category of quality as this category would be filled in during the next stage of the project. An implementation plan was made, and managers were informed about the project and the 13 KPIs. The indicators were programmed into the AZU-score information system. This information system had a dashboard layout. The KPI reporting through AZU-score was integrated into the regular, periodic AZU management reporting. Managers and the board of directors were trained in using the new system and reporting set.

- *Phase 3: Aftercare and maintenance.* In the aftercare phase, the remaining activities regarding implementing certain KPIs were finalized, such as setting up maintenance procedures and adapting the AZU-score system. An evaluation of AZU-score was also made. Main results of this evaluation were: the performance management system did not match needs of the user sufficiently; the KPI reporting was not yet used enough during the daily activities of the managers; and the frequency with which managers made use of the system varied considerably per person and through time. The reason

Exhibit 3.3 **AZU Score KPIs**

Category	KPI	Definition
Patient mix	Referrals	Number of referrals in the referral categories: specialties, reduction of care, and others
	Profile AZU	Proportion of top referrals vs. basic cases of illness
	Management of referral categories	Average difference between planned and actual number of patients per referral category
Cost control	Absenteeism	Absenteeism of employees caused by illness
	Decreased financial budget	Decrease of the yearly financial operating budget, in actuals vs. budget per cumulative month
	Efficiency outpatient clinic	A combination of the number of function studies, repeat visits, laboratory tests, radiation transactions, radio diagnostics, radio therapy, per admission per outpatient clinic per month
	Efficiency clinic	A combination of the number of hospitalization days, function studies, laboratory tests, radiation transactions, radio diagnostics, radio therapy, per admission per clinic per month
Service	Admission time outpatient clinic	Average time elapsed between telephonic contact and first appointment at the clinic
	Telephonic accessibility	Chance of pick up at telephone numbers, important for the accessibility of AZU
	Diagnostic processing time outpatient clinic	Number of diagnostics, per time category of 0–1 day, 2–25 days, and > 25 days after the first appointment at the clinic
	Timeliness clinical letters	Average time elapsed between discharge of patient and sending of clinical letter to patient
	Timeliness outpatient clinical referral letters	Average time elapsed between first appointment at the clinic and sending of referral letter to patient
	Realization surgery hours planning outpatient clinic	Average percentage of difference between planned and actual beginning time of surgery visit + difference between planned and actual ending time of surgery visit versus planned time of visit

for this was that most users had not been involved in the choice of the 13 KPIs (only the board was involved). Increased participation, especially of medical personnel, would help solve this discrepancy. Other results of the evaluation indicated that users missed certain features in AZU-score system, like possibilities for trend analysis, forecasting, and year overviews. As a reaction, the board of directors decided to include the KPIs in the management contracts, which were agreed between each manager and the board each year. In this way, managers would be more or less forced to take notice of the indicators. In addition, it was decided to start the AZU-score II project, which was going to address these issues and which also was going to fill in the quality category.

Results of the AZU Case Study

On the basis of interviews and document research, the behavioral factors were scored for the three stages: (1) starting, (2) development, and (3) use. The criteria for regular use were also scored. In this section, a description is given of the results for AZU.

Starting stage. Within AZU, a positive attitude toward performance management existed at the start of the project. One reason for this was that managers (on all organizational levels) expected that the AZU-score system would give them a better insight into and grip on what was going on in the organization. Second, the chairman of the board of directors expected that managers would start to think more about their performance and how to improve it: "The reporting of KPIs encourages action. At first, people deny the results; but after the reliability of the figures has been shown, they take action." The vice chairman agreed: "Reporting results through AZU-score should help to gain improvements because people become more conscious of problems." Another reason was that many managers had already had experience with performance management at previous employers. Consequently, these managers exhibited a positive expectation at AZU about the performance management system. There was some initial resistance among the medical staff, as one of the medical specialists illustrated: "Medical personnel initially saw the introduction of AZU-score as a shift in power structure: It is a tool to manage them, instead of them managing the tool."

The decision to start with AZU-score was taken exclusively by the board of directors without involvement of the managers. As a consequence, the managers were unclear as to when the project actually had started. For example, dates between 1991 and late 1994 were mentioned even though the project actually started in 1995. The starting time may not have been optimal because at that time a lot of things were going on at AZU. There existed a hectic work situation with a lot of special projects being undertaken, like improving patient satisfaction, defining referral categories, establishing cost prices for medical services, opening of outpatient's clinics, and the integration of AZU with a children's hospital. As a result, the board of directors could not always pay enough attention to the AZU-score project. The conclusion was that the final score for the starting stage at AZU was a 0, which indicates that the behavioral factors for this stage were partially satisfied.

Development stage. The AZU managers were involved only to a small degree in the development of the KPIs. The AZU-score system was initiated by the board of directors, being the main user of the new system. For this reason, the directors chose the KPIs to cover their responsibility areas. The managers received only demonstrations of the system, at which time their reaction and feedback was requested. They did not participate in choosing and defining the KPIs or screen and report layouts or in the setting of targets. This resulted in generic, AZU-wide indicators, which had less relevance for lower levels in the organization because they were not specific enough.

"The developed KPIs are too generic for me to be able to steer the people in my center," stated the manager of the ER Center. And the manager of the OR Center suggested: "AZU-score users should be more involved in defining KPIs and in setting targets for these. This would definitely increase the support basis and the use of the system. Users have the feeling the project team does not know enough what users really need and want."

For this reason, the KPIs did not cover enough of the business activities and the strategic objectives of the divisions, centers, and facilities. Nonetheless, AZU-score system turned out to be a user-friendly system with a clear dashboard, extra information (KPI definitions, relevance of KPI for the strategy, registration, and calculation method) and clear help texts, which helped managers to understand and comprehend quickly the information in the system. AZU-score had a clear internal purpose aimed at supporting internal management, and there was hardly any involvement from external stakeholders.

The conclusion was that the final score for the development stage at AZU was a −, which indicates that the behavioral factors for this stage were insufficiently satisfied.

Use stage. The positive attitude of the AZU managers toward performance management that they displayed at the start of the project was still there after more than one year of use of AZU-score. The results of the KPIs were not threatening as long as the data was reliable and the KPI definitions were solid.

The manager of the OR Center explained: "If results are under target, we call it a crisis and then we work together as a team to solve the problem. For this, we can use the system."

Generating the data needed for the AZU-score system did not cost managers too much effort, and they felt the time allotted to working with the system was reasonable. The information from AZU-score system was seen by a group of managers as steering and managing information, which provided more insight into critical issues.

However, AZU-score system did not seem to be a dynamic management tool: The system did not play a prominent part in the planning and control cycle of AZU, and not all managers used the system regularly. There were several reasons for this. The information from the system was not yet tailored to the various management levels, making it less relevant to the managers. The managers were not involved in making analyses and forecasts, diminishing the added value of the system for supporting the managers in their daily activities. Many managers did not have insight into the relationships between the KPIs themselves and between the KPIs and financial results, making it difficult for them to improve their performance with the help of AZU-score. The board of directors did not visibly use the system themselves, so managers did not know how important the directors considered AZU-score to be for the continuity of AZU. The managers were not held accountable by the board for the KPI results, making the use of AZU-score rather noncommittal. There was no link between AZU-score and the reward structure, diminishing the incentive to improve. Finally, several medical managers stated that the difference between medical and administrative members was an important reason for the lack of use. As a medical specialist commented: "KPIs are often defined differently by medical personnel than by managers. This gives rise to many discussions. Doctors and medical personnel are not used to talking about their work in process terms. For them, numbers and times are not relevant and they should not be held accountable for these. They are raised to think about their work in qualitative terms. Their language is, therefore, quite different from administrative managers. To get the two groups working together better requires a change in language, a change in thinking, and a change in attitude." The manager of Laboratory Center agreed: "AZU-score appeals more to the administrative managers than to the medical staff. The willingness to use the system has to come from the people themselves. However, doctors are more interested in the well-being of their patients than in management issues. This attitude is changing. Now two doctors have become part of the management team: This changes their frame of reference."

The conclusion was that the final score for the use stage at AZU was a 0, which indicates that the behavioral factors for this stage were partially satisfied.

Exhibit 3.4 gives the scores for the behavioral factors in the starting, development, and use stages. For each stage, the final score is also given.

Exhibit 3.4   Behavioral Factor Scores for the Starting, Development, and Use Stages at AZU

Behavioral Factor	Analysis	Score
Starting Stage		
Managers accept the need for performance management.	There was a positive starting attitude toward AZU-score because managers saw the system as necessary for the continuity of the AZU organization.	+
Managers have earlier (positive) experiences with performance management.	There was a positive starting attitude toward AZU-score because many of the managers had previous positive experience with performance management.	+
Managers agree on the starting time.	It was not possible to distill a clear starting point for the project because managers' opinion on this was divided. Their opinion was also divided on the suitability of the starting time of the project.	0
Managers have been involved in decision making about the project start time.	The board of directors took the decision to implement AZU-score; managers were not involved in the decision process.	–
Managers work in a stable, relatively tranquil environment.	At the starting time of the project, there was a turbulent and hectic working situation, caused among other things due to the merger with another hospital.	–
Final score *starting* stage		**0**
Development Stage		
Managers find the performance management system relevant because only those stakeholders interests are incorporated that are important to the organization's success.	The board of supervisors did not have an overriding influence on the development of AZU-score. Consequently, the development of AZU-score was internally focused with some consideration for external requirements.	+

(continues)

Exhibit 3.4 **Continued**

Behavioral Factor	Analysis	Score
Development Stage (continued)		
Managers understand the CSF/KPI/BSC reporting.	AZU-score turned out to be a user-friendly system, with clear help texts, so managers could easily understand the KPI information.	+
Managers understand the meaning of KPIs.	Managers were insufficiently involved in the definition of KPIs. As a consequence, there were regular discussions about KPI meanings, especially between medical and managerial personnel because not all managers had the same knowledge about the KPIs.	0
Managers have insight into the relationship between business processes and CSFs/KPIs.	The relationsip between business processes and CSFs/KPIs was insufficiently crystallized out.	0
Managers can influence the KPIs assigned to them.	Managers were insufficiently involved in the assigning of KPIs to individuals. As a consequence, it was unclear which manager was responsible for which indicator.	0
Managers have insight into the relationship between strategy and CSFs/KPIs.	The KPIs did not match the strategy responsibility of managers completely. In addition, the relationship between strategy and CSFs/KPIs was insufficiently crystallized out.	–
Managers have an active role during the development stage of the performance management system project.	Managers were insufficiently involved in the project. They were informed through (voluntary) presentations, where sometimes their feedback was asked on certain issues.	–
Managers are involved in defining KPIs.	Managers were not involved in the definition of KPIs. Their opinion was asked about indicators that were previously defined by the project team.	–
Managers are involved in setting KPI targets.	Managers were not involved in target setting. This was, among other things, because (initially) targets were only set for three of the thirteen KPIs.	–
Managers' KPI sets are aligned with their responsibility areas.	The KPI sets did insufficiently match the responsibility areas of the managers. Several indicators were missing in the sets of the divisional and center managers.	–
Managers are involved in making the CSF/KPI/BSC report layout.	Managers were not involved in making the report layout. Their opinion was asked on layouts that were previously defined by the project team.	–

Exhibit 3.4 **Continued**

Behavioral Factor	Analysis	Score
Development Stage (continued)		
Managers use the CSFs/KPIs/BSC that match their responsibility areas.	Managers were insufficiently involved in the assigning of KPIs to individuals. No formal accountability setting between board and managers took place.	–
Managers accept the promoter.	The organization did not recognize a clear project sponsor.	–
Managers are actively communicating about the performance management system project.	There was insufficient data to be able to judge this.	NA
Managers are informed about the status of the performance management system project.	There was insufficient data to be able to judge this.	NA
Managers' information processing capabilities are not exceeded by the number of CSFs/KPIs.	There was insufficient data to be able to judge this.	NA
Managers see the promoter spends enough time on the performance management system implementation.	There was insufficient data to be able to judge this.	NA
Managers find the performance management system relevant because it has a clear internal control purpose.	There was insufficient data to be able to judge this.	NA
Final score *development* stage		–
Use Stage		
Managers do not get discouraged by the collection of performance data.	Less than 25% of the data had to be collected manually, making the collecting and reporting of the KPIs very efficient.	+
Managers have enough time to work with their CSFs/KPIs/BSC.	On the one hand, it did not take managers too much time to work with AZU-score due due to the ease of operation. On the other hand, managers have enough time to work with the system, as part of their daily activities.	+

(continues)

Exhibit 3.4   **Continued**

Behavioral Factor	Analysis	Score
Use Stage (continued)		
Managers do not experience CSFs/KPIs/BSC as threatening.	The results of AZU-score were not considered to be threatening by the managers. Managers communicated in positive terms about the AZU-score system.	+
Managers' results on CSFs/KPIs/BSC are openly communicated.	All users had access to all the information in the system (i.e., every KPI for AZU total and the individual divisions).	+
Managers' activities are supported by KPIs.	Managers who used the system stated they gained a better insight into critical issues and bottlenecks, and also had a better basis for their decision and action taking.	+
Managers trust the performance information.	There were many discussions about the reliability of the KPI results, caused by the limited insight of managers into the underlying data and by insufficient registration of important data by various divisions/departments. This unreliability was sometimes used as an excuse for not using the AZU-score system. From a more objective viewpoint, the data appeared to be quite reliable.	0
Managers are involved in making analyses.	Analyses were irregularly made during work meetings, on the spot, by the managers.	0
Managers trust good-quality analyses.	The analyses were open and transparent. However, these analyses were only made infrequently, which did not improve their quality.	0
Managers use the performance management system regularly during the planning and control cycle.	Just after the time of the case study, the information from AZU-score would become a standard discussion item during the quarterly meetings between the board of directors and managers (no + was awarded because this was not a reality yet).	0
Managers realize the importance of CSFs/KPIs/BSC to their performance.	Managers, who used AZU-score irregularly, sometimes had difficulty seeing how they could improve their performance on the KPIs.	0
Managers have insight into the relationship between KPIs and financial results.	A direct and clear relationship between KPIs and financial results was lacking, caused among others by inaccurate cost prices of medical services.	−

Exhibit 3.4 **Continued**

Behavioral Factor	Analysis	Score
Use Stage (continued)		
Managers have insight into the relationship between cause and effect.	Managers did not (yet) think structurally about the relationship between KPI results and the causes for these results.	–
Managers are involved in forecasting.	Forecasts were generated automatically by the AZU-score system, based on certain mathematical algorithms. Managers were not involved in making forecasts.	–
Managers find the performance management system relevant due to regular evaluations.	There were irregular evaluations of the relevance of the KPIs in AZU-score.	–
Managers agree on changes in the CSF/KPI set.	Managers would make suggestions for changes in AZU-score, but these were only implemented sparsely.	–
Managers' use of the performance management system is stimulated by the reward structure.	There was no formal link between managers' performance on AZU-score and the rewards of managers.	–
Managers clearly see the promoter using the performance management system.	The use of AZU-score by the board of directors was not very visible to the organization; many managers did not know how important the directors considered the performance management system to be.	–
Managers and their controlling systems have a mutual trust.	There was insufficient data to be able to judge this.	NA
Managers are stimulated to improve their performance.	There was insufficient data to be able to judge this.	NA
Managers trust good-quality forecasts.	There was insufficient data to be able to judge this.	NA
Managers can use their CSFs/KPIs/BSC for managing their employees.	There was insufficient data to be able to judge this.	NA
Managers have sole responsibility for a KPI.	There was insufficient data to be able to judge this.	NA
Managers' information processing capabilities are not exceeded by the number of CSFs/KPIs.	There was insufficient data to be able to judge this.	NA
Final score *use* stage		**0**

Criteria for regular use.   Exhibit 3.5 gives the scores for the criteria for
regular use, which indicate whether the implementation of the new
AZU-score system can be considered to be successful.

The use of AZU-score system could not yet be called an unqualified
success. Although most managers had a positive attitude about the system, it seemed to have more value for the board of directors than for the
divisional, center, and facility managers. As one of the managers commented: "The sponsor has a performance management way of thinking,
which is very important for a project like this. This means that, to make
AZU-score a real success, a change in culture and a similar management
style [to that of the sponsor] is required." The chairman of the board elu-

Exhibit 3.5   Criteria for Regular Use Scores for AZU

Criteria for Regular Use	*Analysis*	*Score*
Plans for follow-up projects	There were plans for further development of AZU-score, called AZU-score II.	+
CSFs, KPIs, and BSC incorporated in the regular management reporting	CSFs and KPIs were incorporated in the formal management reporting to the managers.	+
Organizational results improved, objectively	The results of AZU were slightly improved since the start of the project.	0
Increased performance management system use by managers	Managers differed about the degree of use of the AZU-score system, some used the system more, others less. Available system documentation indicated a slight decrease in performance management system use.	0
Difference in attitude toward performance management, between project start and currently	There was not a great difference in attitude toward AZU-score, between project start and the time of the study.	0
Regular communication about KPI results	Managers differed about the degree of communication about the KPI results. There was structured communication during the quarterly meetings, but apart from that there was little communication among managers about AZU-score.	0
Organizational results improved, through performance management system use	Managers differed about the degree of improvement caused specifically by the use of AZU-score. Many managers doubted there were any improvements.	–
Final score criteria for regular use		**0**

cidated: "In a professional organization like AZU, the emphasis in the management style lies on communication, the strength of your arguments, and on consensus. The board has to be a supervisor, coach, and mentor at the same time. Team work is crucial. To support this, a system like AZU-score is needed and by using the system themselves, the board of directors shows the organization that the system and its use is important." Communication about the results of AZU-score varied quite a bit: Officially, the results were discussed during the quarterly meetings between directors and managers, but the questionnaire showed that 60% of the managers spoke on average less than once a month about the AZU-score results. In addition, the performance of the organization had not significantly improved through the use of AZU-score. Reasons for this were the lack of relevant divisional, center, and facility indicators, and the relative newness of the system, which still contained data that was considered to be unreliable.

Meanwhile, the first steps have been taken to improve the system, by starting with project AZU-score II, which will refine the current KPIs and also add new ones (for the quadrant quality). The outcome of this project will most probably determine if the implementation of a performance management system at AZU turns out to be a worthwhile effort. The chairman of the board promised a change in approach for this new project: "In the AZU-score II project, medical personnel and doctors will be more involved to prevent conflicts between them and administrative managers."

The conclusion was that the final score for the criteria for regular use at AZU was a 0, which indicates that the implementation of AZU-score was a partial success.

KADASTER

The Kadaster is the land registry office of the Netherlands. The organization collects, accepts, mutates, maintains, and provides information about immovable property and real estate; processes license and act requests for property transfers and mutations; collaborates in the planning of land use; and maintains the network of coordination points that is used while surveying the land. The Kadaster has branches in 15 towns, which are profit centers.

The reason to perform case study research at Kadaster was twofold. First, Kadaster had, at the time of the case study, already worked with a performance management system called control-variables for over three years. There were 80 users. Second, the strategy of Kadaster indicated that the organization wanted to have a pivotal position in the capturing and distributing property and real estate information. To be able to better achieve this position, the Kadaster was transformed from a governmental agency to an independent agency, giving the organization more freedom. This meant the performance management system had been developed as part of a major organizational change and was now used in a holding structure; the control-variables were specifically used by the head office in managing the profit centers. In this environment of change, behavioral factors may turn out to play a big role.

Description of Kadaster

The organizational structure of the Kadaster consists of a board of directors, holding staff, 15 branches (profit centers) and the Center of Information and Geodetic Technology (IGT). Each branch consists, among other things, of the departments Real Estate Information (REI), Land Surveyors (LS), Legal Affairs, and Controlling. The Kadaster has a fair number of external stakeholders: the Minister of Housing, Planning, and Environment; the board of supervisors; the unions; and a user council (Exhibit 3.6). Each branch has its own internal management reporting for internal control. This branch reporting is used as the basis for reporting to the head office.

In 1991, a new concept for the planning and control cycle was introduced at Kadaster. As a logical consequence of this new concept, the first ideas about a performance management system were suggested. In 1992, the definition of critical success factors (CSFs) and KPIs (at Kadaster called control-variables, or CVs) started, and at the beginning of 1993, these were implemented. In 1994, Kadaster was turned into an independent agency. At the time of the case study research, 1997, Kadaster was reorganizing, adjusting the workforce in numbers and skills to better match the new status and activities of the organization.

The performance management system project was executed in several steps:

- *Step 1:* Defining the CSFs on the basis of Kadaster's strategy.
- *Step 2:* Defining the criteria for the CVs. These should become part of the regular reporting from branches to head office. The idea was initially that each management level should have its own CV set. These sets would match the various responsibility areas: a strategic set for the board of directors, a tactical set for the branch managers, and an operational set for branch department heads. These sets

Exhibit 3.6 Simplified Organizational Structure of Kadaster

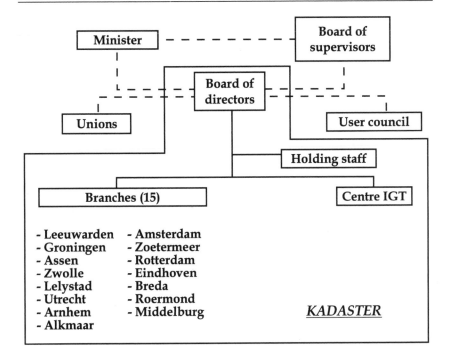

would be defined with participation from various management levels. The CV set would be adjusted as soon as the strategy, business processes, or CSFs changed. The organization decided to first start developing the CVs for the strategic set. These CVs would then all (in time) be reported by each branch to the board. The following set was defined by a project team and presented for approval during the central management team meeting (Exhibit 3.7).

- *Step 3:* Defining the chosen CVs. This included defining the source of data for the CV, frequency of reporting, the organizational unit for which the CV had to be reported, and report layouts (Exhibit 3.8).

  The CVs were defined in such a way that the target for each CV and for each branch was put on 100. Through this indexing, the branches could be made comparable, irrespective of the actual volumes at the branches (Exhibit 3.9).

- *Step 4:* Translating the strategic CVs to the tactical and operational levels (at the departments and branches). A first setup was made by one of the holding staff departments. The branches were supposed to refine the setup further and complete the definitions for their

Exhibit 3.7   **Kadaster's CVs**

CSF	CV	Comment
Cost coverage and solvability	None	The current reports (Profit & Loss, Balance Sheet, Total Budget Overview) provide all the financial information that is needed. No additional CVs are needed.
Expense coverage	None	The current report (Liquidity Planning) provides the information that is needed. No additional CVs are needed.
Quality of service	Throughput time mass output	The average time it takes to process license/act requests.
	Authorization time	The average authorization time of license/act requests.
	Work inventory license/act requests	The average work backlog, in numbers, of license/act requests.
	Age license/ act requests	The average elapsed waiting time (before processing takes place) of license/act requests.
Efficiency	Productivity	The number of processed license/act requests vs. number of personnel.
	Other activities departments REI and LS	Time spent on other activities vs. time spent on productive activities. For the departments REI and LS, this ratio is reported, in order to make sure no transfer of hours takes place to the category "other activities," to boost performance.
	Direct personnel costs department REI	Sales turnover vs. actual production costs.
Entrepreneurship	Other costs	Sales turnover vs. other costs. If sales turnover decreases, other costs should also decrease.
	Open Accounts Receivable	The average elapsed time between sending out and collecting on accounts receivable.
Workforce	Various human resource CVs	These human resource CVs were going to be developed at a later stage and have not been included in the case study.
Competitive position	None	At the time of the case study research, no CVs had been developed yet for this CSF.

CVs; however, this did not happen. This is why no examples of these reports can be given here.

- *Step 5:* Evaluation of the current CV sets. Several recalibrated CV sets were the result of this evaluation. These sets were going to be implemented in 1998 (after the time of the case study).

Results of the Kadaster Case Study

On the basis of interviews and document research, the behavioral factors were scored for the three stages: (1) starting, (2) development, and (3) use. In addition, the criteria for regular use were scored. In this section, a description is given of the results for Kadaster.

Starting stage. Within Kadaster, a positive attitude toward performance management existed at the start of the project despite the fact that most managers did not have any previous experience with performance management. This was because managers viewed the performance management system as being important for the continuity of the newly formed independent agency. The CVs would make it possible for them to get insight into issues and bottlenecks of the new processes and strategy execution. As the controller at the head office put it: "The advantages of the CVs are that they limit the volume of management reporting, focus attention on a limited set of critical issues, make standardization of reporting over all branches possible, and structure the discussions between the branches and the board." A branch manager commented: "The advantage of the CVs is that they are a tool to get a better grip on the execution of the strategy. The disadvantage is that they create a degree of pressure: You have the feeling the CVs urge you to become more productive all the time."

The managers at the branches and departments could spend only limited time on the project because they had their hands full with the transition to the new organizational setup and the corresponding change process. The head office took the responsibility for developing and proposing the new indicators.

The conclusion was that the final score for the starting stage at Kadaster was a +, which indicates that most of the behavioral factors for this stage were satisfied.

Development stage. Involvement of managers during the development stage was limited. The CVs have been identified at head office with the board of directors as the premier user group. The CVs were then more or less forced on the branch managers. This was a conscious decision of the

Exhibit 3.8 **Branch Report Example (Translated from Dutch)**

Profit & Loss Account	Internal Report				Branch xxxx	
	Month		Cumulative		Year Plan	
	NLG	% vs. Total Branch Turnover	NLG	% vs. Total Branch Turnover	NLG	% vs. Total Branch Turnover
Branch Turnover:						
Statutory activities	1323	80%	4059	77%	14301	87%
Market activities	311	19%	691	13%	2088	13%
Mutation work inventory	20	1%	520	10%	0	0%
Production own account	0	0%	0	0%	0	0%
Total branch turnover	1654	100%	5270	100%	16388	100%
Branch Costs:						
Salaries	724	44%	2160	41%	8580	52%
Social premium costs	62	4%	186	4%	700	4%
Depreciation	75	5%	223	4%	795	5%
Mutation provisions	−252	−15%	−527	−10%	−801	−5%
Outsourced work	408	25%	803	15%	2541	16%
Other branch costs	464	28%	1350	26%	5626	34%
Allocated overhead (from Center IGT)	0	0%	0	0%	0	0%
Total branch costs	1481	90%	4195	80%	17441	106%

	Month		Cumulative			
Branch turnover—costs	173	10%	1075	20%	−1053	−6%
Turnover claims	−1	0%	−2	0%	−6	0%
Result regular branch activities	172	10%	1073	0%	−1059	−6%
Extraordinary income	0	0%	0	0%	0	0%
Result branch	172	10%	1073	20%	−1059	−6%

Control Variables	*Month*	*Cumulative*	*Year Plan*
Absenteeism:			
Management team	0.0	0.0	4.0
Department Controlling	8.9	11.1	4.0
Department LS	6.0	7.7	4.0
Department REI	3.5	2.8	4.0

Exhibit 3.9 **Indexed CV Report, Showing Results for All Branches (Translated from Dutch)**

Branch	Productivity Real Estate Information					Productivity Land Surveyors				
	1993	1994	1995	1996	1997	1993	1994	1995	1996	1997
Groningen	95	94	101	101		106	98	101	96	
Leeuwarden	107	92	98	98		109	96	97	98	
Assen	103	99	106	107		113	99	102	101	
Zwolle	96	107	103	102		101	105	102	100	
Arnhem	95	99	101	100		103	95	103	104	
Utrecht	105	102	102	108		108	97	101	103	
Lelystad	135	101	99	93		155	91	98	99	
Alkmaar	102	103	98	104		109	99	96	97	
Amsterdam	102	105	96	96		99	104	102	105	
Zoetermeer	—	93	102	101		104	98	102	99	
Rotterdam	115	98	105	105		91	97	98	99	
Middelburg	144	107	99	100		113	95	98	98	
Eindhoven	106	110	100	103		106	100	93	99	
Breda	94	104	98	92		104	102	97	98	
Roermond	98	87	98	98		87	99	94	98	
Average	107	100	100	101		107	98	99	100	

head office because the branch managers had to concentrate on the transition to the independent agency status and could not afford to spend (too much) time on the CV project. The directors regarded the CVs as being especially useful in their accountability toward the board of supervisors, although this board did not have any influence on the type of CVs being developed. The directors initially thought the CVs would be less relevant for the internal control of the branches because this would entail further tailoring of the CVs to local circumstances. The head office suggested that the branches take the initiative in this regard, which most of them did. A branch director suggested: "During the development of CVs, people in the branches should be more involved. The CV method is a good one, but not always an easy one. To let people better understand it, they should be educated and should be involved in discussions and in defining the indicators."

At the time of the CV development, there was a clear relation between strategy, CSFs, and CVs. However, in three years' time, the circumstances of Kadaster had changed and for this reason the organization's strategy had been adapted. Unfortunately, the CVs had not been updated and, therefore, started to become less relevant for both board and managers. Kadaster had at the time of the case study research just decided to make an evaluation and an update of the CVs.

The conclusion was that the final score for the development stage at Kadaster was a 0, which indicates that the behavioral factors for this stage were partially satisfied.

Use stage.   All the management levels used the CVs, especially at branch and department levels. According to a member of the board of directors: "A precondition for good use of CVs is having the discipline to only look at the exceptions, being CVs of target, giving freedom to the branches to manage using the CVs, and visible use by the board by challenging the branches on their CV results."

The role of the board of directors had become more passive in this respect, which sometimes had a detrimental effect on the quality of the CV discussion meetings between directors and branch managers. The employees did not recognize the value of the CVs, probably because their exposure to the indicators had been limited up to now. The results of the CVs were not regarded as threatening because they were clearly listed for all 15 branches and were available for everybody. Sometimes, they were even put on bulletin boards. This was possible because there existed a good relationship between the board and the branches. The culture at Kadaster was characterized as being open, focusing on improvement and a loose control environment. A reason for this was, as a board member put it: "The open culture at Kadaster is possible because the CVs cannot be manipulated." Nonetheless, there was a clear accountability tree, including directors who spoke to branch managers about CV results, branch managers who spoke to department heads, and department heads who spoke to their staff. Important to keep in mind, according to a branch manager, was that "CVs alone are not enough, you have to know the story behind them. This is especially important if you discuss your results with the board, otherwise the board may be inclined to judge you too fast." The conclusion was that the final score for the use stage at Kadaster was a +, which indicates that the behavioral factors for this stage were mostly satisfied.

Exhibit 3.10 gives the scores for the behavioral factors in the starting, development, and use stages. For each stage the final score is also given.

Exhibit 3.10   **Behavioral Factors Scores, for the Starting, Development, and Use Stages at Kadaster**

Behavioral Factor	Analysis	Score
Starting Stage		
Managers accept the need for performance management.	There was a positive starting attitude toward the performance management system because managers recognized that such a system was needed in order to be able, as a newly independent agency, to achieve the objectives and targets.	+
Managers have earlier (positive) experiences with performance management.	Managers did not have earlier experience with performance management, but nonetheless they had a positive attitude toward CSFs and CVs.	+
Managers agree on the starting time.	Managers viewed the performance management system as a logical part of the new planning and control concept, so the starting point was considered to be well chosen.	+
Managers work in a stable, relatively tranquil environment.	There was a turbulent work situation in the organization because Kadaster was changing, at that moment, to an independent agency. However, because the CVs were not developed by managers at the branches or departments but by a project team at the head office, the branches were not too much affected by the CV project.	0

Exhibit 3.10   Continued

Behavioral Factor	Analysis	Score
Starting Stage (continued)		
Managers have been involved in decision making around the project start time.	The board of directors took the decision to implement a performance management system; branch managers were not involved.	−
Final score *starting* stage		+
Development Stage		
Managers find the performance management system relevant because it has a clear internal control purpose.	The CV report was set up with a clear internal management control purpose.	+
Managers find the performance management system relevant because only those stakeholders' interests are incorporated that are important to the organization's success.	External stakeholders were not involved in the development and, therefore, did not direct the content of the CV set. Only for the external stakeholder critical information was included.	+
Managers have insight into the relationship between strategy and CSFs/KPIs.	At the time of development, there was a clear relationship between strategy, CSFs and CVs. However, the CV set had not been evaluated and updated since then, so it was felt by the organization that the strategic relevance of the set could be less.	0
Managers have insight into the relationship between business processes and CSFs/KPIs.	Opinions were divided about the degree to which the CVs represented the crucial activities sufficiently.	0
Managers are involved in setting KPI targets.	Head office set targets for all CVs; branch managers were involved in a limited way.	0
Managers' KPI sets are aligned with their responsibility areas.	At head office, CVs were successfully developed for the board of directors. The development of the tactical and operational CVs was left to the branches themselves with varying success.	0
Managers understand the CSF/KPI/BSC reporting.	The quarterly reporting for the board of directors had a standardized format, which was easy to understand. The branches could make their own layouts, which were difficult to understand for others (like the board and other branches). This was a drawback because the CV reports were used for benchmarking.	0

(continues)

Exhibit 3.10 **Continued**

Behavioral Factor	Analysis	Score
Development Stage (continued)		
Managers use the CSFs/KPIs/BSC that match their responsibility areas.	The developed CVs covered the responsibility areas of the board of directors. They provided limited coverage of the responsibility areas of managers because the CV reports were not tailored at all branches.	0
Managers accept the promoter.	During the interviews several persons were mentioned as possibly being the project sponsor. The sponsor was low key and not really known in the organization.	0
Managers see that the promoter spends enough time on the performance management system implementation.	The sponsor (a board member) regularly spent (limited) time with the project team.	0
Managers have an active role during the development stage of the performance management system project.	The CVs were developed by the project team in discussions with the board of directors. It was a centrally led project. Branch managers were not involved in the development stage.	–
Managers are involved in making the CSF/KPI/BSC report layout.	The design and layout of the CV reports were developed by the project team. Branch managers were not involved in the development stage.	–
Managers are involved in defining KPIs.	The CVs were developed by the project team. It was a centrally led project. Branch managers were not involved in the development stage.	–
Managers can influence the KPIs assigned to them.	The final choice of CVs was made by the board of directors. The branch managers were not involved.	–
Managers are informed about the status of the performance management system project.	Managers were not informed about the status of the CV project. No discussions took place about the relevance, added value, and desired indicators.	–
Managers are actively communicating about the performance management system project.	There was insufficient data to be able to judge this.	NA
Managers understand the meaning of KPIs.	There was insufficient data to be able to judge this.	NA

Exhibit 3.10   **Continued**

Behavioral Factor	*Analysis*	*Score*
Development Stage (continued)		
Final score *development* stage		**0**
Use Stage		
Managers are stimulated to improve their performance.	There was an open, trusting atmosphere and culture in the organization. Everybody was striving toward continuous improvement.	+
Managers' results on CSFs/KPIs/BSC are openly communicated.	There was great openness about the CV results. CV results from all branches were collected and reported together on a ranking list. In some branches the results were put on the bulletin board.	+
Managers and their controlling systems have a mutual trust.	The relationship between board of directors and branch managers was characterized as mutual trust. There was loose control from the board toward the branches.	+
Managers realize the importance of CSFs/KPIs/ BSC to their performance.	Managers recognized the importance of the CVs in supporting their daily activities.	+
Managers do not get discouraged by the collection of performance data.	Less than 25% of the required data for the CVs had to be collected manually. This was deemed quite acceptable by the managers.	+
Managers' frames of reference contain similar KPIs.	A frame of reference was created for the managers through the ranking list: the comparison of the 15 branches on their CV results.	+
Managers are involved in making analyses.	The managers made analyses as soon as actual CV results deviated from the targets.	+
Managers have enough time to work with their CSFs/ KPIs/BSC.	The time spent by managers working on their CVs varied from 30 minutes to several days per month. In general, managers were of the opinion they could spend enough time on working with the CVs.	+
Managers do not experience CSFs/KPIs/BSC as threatening.	Performance management was not experienced as being threatening. There was an open culture at Kadaster, aimed at improvement.	+

(continues)

Exhibit 3.10   **Continued**

Behavioral Factor	Analysis	Score
Use Stage (continued)		
Managers can use their CSFs/KPIs/BSC for managing their employees.	Managers recognized many advantages in using CVs while managing their subordinates, like the structuring of discussions and the quick gaining of insight into employees' performance.	+
Managers have insight into the relationship between KPIs and financial results.	The relationships between CVs and financial results were not identified nor quantified. However, through the use of the CVs, these relationships were starting to be discerned (implicitly) by the managers.	0
Managers' activities are supported by KPIs.	The CVs supported the managers in their daily activities. Managers formulated and undertook actions, if necessary. However, these actions were not recorded in the management reporting and could, therefore, not be checked by me (consequently, a 0 was awarded instead of a +).	0
Managers trust the performance information.	The reliability of the CVs had greatly improved compared to the starting stage. However, still many discussions took place, not about the reliability of the data, but about the reliability and accuracy of the CV definitions.	0
Managers trust good-quality analyses.	The analyses were in general open and issues surfaced. However, these analyses were not recorded in the management reporting and could, therefore, not be checked by me (consequently, a 0 was awarded instead of a +).	0
Managers have sole responsibility for a KPI.	There was a clear accountability for each KPI. The branch manager was responsible for the CVs in his or her branch, he or she would appoint department heads. Whether this appointment of accountability took place was unclear to me.	0
Managers clearly see the promoter using the performance management system.	The board of directors discussed the CVs every quarter with the branch managers, sometimes on a high level, sometimes very detailed. There was no evidence the board used the system more often.	0

Exhibit 3.10   **Continued**

Behavioral Factor	Analysis	Score
Use Stage (continued)		
Managers have insight into the relationship between cause and effect.	The CVs were developed with the board in mind; therefore, branch managers could not (directly) see the relationship between cause and effect for their own activities.	–
Managers are involved in forecasting.	Within the organization, there was no clarity about the nature of forecasting, i.e., what a forecast was. As a consequence, none were made.	–
Managers find the performance management system relevant due to regular evaluations.	Five years after developing the draft CV set, the first formal evaluation took place. The fact that this evaluation took place was not known at the branches.	–
Managers use the performance management system regularly during the planning and control cycle.	The CVs were not a formal part of the planning and control cycle at Kadaster.	–
Managers agree on changes in the CSF/KPI set.	Suggestions for changes in the CV set were not regularly collected. Branch managers felt that if they did make suggestions, no follow-up took place.	–
Managers' use of the performance management system is stimulated by the reward structure.	Results on CVs were not formally linked to the reward structure.	–
Managers' information processing capabilities are not exceeded by the number of CSFs/KPIs.	There was insufficient data to be able to judge this.	NA
Managers trust good-quality forecasts.	There was insufficient data to be able to judge this.	NA
Final score *use* stage		+

Criteria for regular use.   Exhibit 3.11 gives the scores for the criteria for regular use, which indicate whether the implementation of the CVs can be considered to be successful.

The use of the CVs in Kadaster can be called successful. Managers still had, after three years of use, a positive feeling about performance management and the use of the indicators was stable. A board member had an interesting point of view on the use of CVs: "Kadaster had a handicap while introducing the CVs: The financial results were so good that CVs were considered to be less important for the continuity of the organization. Several 'bad' years would be good for the use of the CVs." A branch manager agreed: "If the results on the CVs would be worse than they are now, then the indicators would receive more attention."

The organization had worked on improving the performance management system: The reliability of the CVs had improved, a more struc-

Exhibit 3.11   Criteria for Regular Use Scores for Kadaster

Criteria for Regular Use	Analysis	Score
Organizational results improved, through the performance management system use	The performance on the CVs had clearly improved since 1993.	+
Increased performance management system used by managers	Use, measured in time spent on the CVs, had stayed the same. However, managers were of the opinion that their use had become more efficient.	+
Difference in attitude toward performance management, between project start and currently	The attitude of managers toward the CVs was positive, both at the starting point as at the time of the study.	+
Regular communication about KPI results	Every month and quarter the CV results were discussed.	+
CSFs, KPIs, and BSC incorporated in the regular management reporting	The CVs were part of the internal, regular management reporting.	+
Organizational results improved, objectively	Opinions were divided about whether the CVs had actually helped in improving organizational performance.	0
Plans for follow-up projects	About half of the managers knew about follow-up plans for the performance management system.	0
Final score criteria for regular use		+

tured discussion about CV content and results took place, and the added value of the CV reporting was clearly seen in the organization. On top of this, at the time of the case study research, a recalibration of the CVs took place, to make sure the CV set would be relevant (again). The CV reporting was seen as a "living management tool" in Kadaster. The conclusion was that the final score for the criteria for regular use at Kadaster was a +, which indicates that the implementation of the CVs was a success.

EUROPEAN IT SERVICES

European Information Services (EIS)[2] is part of a multinational organization in the oil industry. It was created in January 1997, when the organization merged with the central information services department of the head office. EIS delivers IT products (hardware and software) and services to all the group companies. The unit is located in the Netherlands, with representatives at sites in the United Kingdom.

The reasons to perform case study research at EIS was twofold. First of all, two departments of EIS had, at the time of the case study, more than one year of experience with a performance management system based on CSFs and KPIs. Second, EIS had used a uniform development approach in both departments, so the expectation was that these departments would be well comparable.

Description of EIS

EIS consists of seven units (Exhibit 3.12). Five of these units provide services to customers at the sites of the oil company, and two units provide supporting services to these five units and to the EIS management team. The case study research focuses on two departments in the Finance & Planning (F&P) unit, which consists of five departments. The Financial Accounting (FA) department provides financial accounting support to EIS locally at the sites, after which consolidation in the Netherlands takes place. The Commercial Services (CS) department provides procurement support of IT products and services from third parties on behalf of the EIS sites.

The mission of Finance & Planning reads as follows: "To deliver information and services to European IT Services' companies, at agreed levels of quality and cost." The FA department supported this mission by the strategy: "Providing financial accounting support in a professional manner such that the company's internal and external obligations are met in the most cost-effective manner, the control framework of the financial

Exhibit 3.12   **Simplified Organizational Structure of EIS**

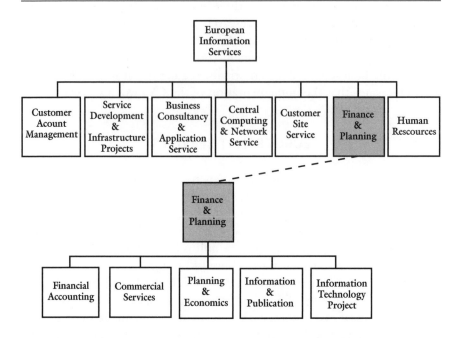

accounting processes is in place and operating, and internal and external customers recognize and value financial accounting's contribution to the businesses." The CS department supported this mission by the following strategies: "Procure goods and services at optimal levels of quality and cost by negotiating in joint teams of technical (from the unit departments) and commercial staff (commercial services) in order to obtain the optimal balance in 'the best technical solution for the best commercial arrangement' considering the 'total cost of ownership'; obtaining maximum economy of scales by applying master contracts; employing quality staff in the CS department, consisting of negotiators who are acknowledged specialists in (the procurement of) products and services, and supporting staff who are pro-active; and communicating CS services, expertise, and results to the EIS organization."

During 1995, several projects were undertaken at EIS. The FA department conducted a project to strengthen the financial controls, which were in place at the EIS organization. The CS department developed a new procurement business model. Following these projects, both departments started with the development of CSFs and KPIs.

The project kicked off with formulating the strategy and mapping out the most important (crucial) business activities of each department. Then, for the strategy and for each crucial business activity, one CSF was selected so that all important strategic and operational activities in the department are covered. After that, one or two KPIs were selected for each CSF. In this way, the total number of indicators was kept within limits. For each KPI, one so-called KPI-custodian was appointed. Then, it was determined whether or not there was a relationship between the KPIs in the set. After all, the performance on one KPI can influence the performance on another KPI—positively or negatively.

Finally, a target was set for each KPI. Exhibit 3.13 gives some examples of the developed CSFs and KPIs.

Exhibit 3.13   **CSFs and KPIs for the FA and CS Departments Examples**

Critical Success Factor	Key Performance Indicator	Definition
Financial Accounting Department		
Professionalism	Functional Training	The number of relevant courses followed versus the number of employees
Timetable compliance	Variation in days on timetable	Number of days overdue or number of days underdue compared with the timetable for closing the general ledger and generating cost reports per month
Invoices paid in agreed terms	Invoices paid on time	Number of invoices paid in the agreed time frame divided by the total number of invoices paid per month
Payments received in agreed terms	Overdue outstanding balance	Overdue outstanding balance per month divided by the total amount of invoices issued in the previous three months
Project capacity	Time spent on specific projects	Total time staff spent on specific improvement/cost reduction projects divided by the total budgeted work time of staff
Control framework compliance	Solved audit points	Total number of audit points solved in the reporting period vs. the total number of audit points that are open and due year-to-date per quarter

(continues)

Exhibit 3.13 **Continued**

Critical Success Factor	Key Performance Indicator	Definition
Financial Accounting Department (continued)		
Efficient invoice process	Processing time for an invoice	The total work time needed (in hours) for processing all invoices registered per month divided by the total number of invoices paid per month
Timeliness of invoice payment	Payment lead time	Average number of days between invoice receipt date and date of payment vs. the total number of invoices paid per month
Quality of billing	Credit notes	Total amount of credit notes per month divided by the total amount of proceeds of the previous month and the reporting month
Informed customer	Inquiries about invoices	Number of inquiries about invoices per month divided by the total number of charging records of the two months previous to the reporting month
Up-to-date asset registers	Book-to-physical	Number of mismatches in the asset registers per quarter
Quality of reports	Number of complaints about reports	Number of formal complaints by management about reports per quarter
Commercial Services Department		
Joint technical/ commercial teams	Joint technical/ commercial teams involved in commercial issues	Number of commercial issues handled by joint technical and commercial teams divided by the total number of commercial issues
Technical/ Commercial balance	Clients' satisfaction on commercial issue outcomes	Sum of the ratings from clients on commercial issue outcomes divided by the total number of commercial issues for which a rating was given
Master contract	Master contract coverage [numbers]	Number of master contracts concluded since January 1 in the current year divided by the total number of contracts concluded since January 1 this current year

Exhibit 3.13 **Continued**

Critical Success Factor	Key Performance Indicator	Definition
Commercial Services Department (continued)		
Master contract	Master contract coverage [value]	Total spending under master contracts since January 1 in the current year, divided by the total EIS procurement spending since January 1 this current year
Quality personnel	Training days	Total number of training days attended by CS staff since January 1 in the current year divided by the total number of training days planned for CS since January 1 this current year
Proactiveness	Commercial opportunities	Average number of commercial opportunities recognized and offered to the client, over all departments
Timeliness	Request for service response time (I)	Average throughput time from raising a request to the last approval by CS
Timeliness	Request for service response time (II)	Average throughput time from the approval to the closing date of the request
Up-to-date contracts	Deadlines met	Number of contracts for which the expiration date or review date has exceeded with action (renewal or termination) taken, divided by the total number of expired or reviewed contracts
Reliability of the database	Complaints about the database	Total number of formal complaints about the contents of the database
Standardization	Standardization initiatives	Number of standardization initiatives started or successfully implemented since January 1 in the current year

The time needed for the implementation of the performance management system was three months, of which 50 working days were spent on the development of the CSFs and the KPIs. The activities were mainly performed by a project team of outside consultants, whereby discussions frequently took place with the head of the FA unit, department heads, and employees. After the project, both the FA and the CS department started to use a finance and a commercial services (procurement) CSF/KPI report respectively.

Results of the EIS Case Study

On the basis of interviews and document research, the behavioral factors were scored separately for each of the two departments, for the three stages: (1) starting, (2) development, and (3) use. The criteria for regular use were also scored. These scores were discussed with the manager F&P and both department heads (CS and FA). In this section, a description is given of the results for the two departments of EIS.

Starting stage. Managers from the FA and the CS departments had a positive attitude at the start of the CSF/KPI project. This positive attitude was caused by the fact that managers considered the use of CSFs and KPIs to be a logical next step after the financial control project. With the implementation of CSFs and KPIs, managers expected to be better able to monitor the implementation and use of the controls and if efficiency and effectiveness gains were obtained. As the FA department head elaborated: "KPIs are useful because you can easily see what is going on inside your department. People inside the department have the tendency to 'work in circles.' They sometimes do not see where they are going. The use of KPIs gives them a more structured approach and a clear direction to where they are going." Apart from that, the managers all had positive previous experiences with performance measurement, which had a positive influence on the attitude and image forming toward the CSF/KPI project. The managers were also actively involved in the decision-making process of the CSF/KPI project. However, they could not spend enough time on the development of the CSFs and KPIs due to the busy, turbulent working situation at EIS at that time, ongoing projects, and the yearly close that took place simultaneously during the project.

The conclusion was that the final score for the starting stage at EIS was a +, which indicates that most of the behavioral factors for this stage were satisfied.

Development stage. Managers were actively involved in the development of the CSFs and KPIs through participating in workshops and project meetings. The promoter of the CSF/KPI project consciously delegated the project tasks to the responsible managers inside the departments. The involvement of these managers had a positive influence on their understanding of the KPI definitions and the new management report. In addition, the managers accepted responsibilities for the KPI results because they recognized a clear relationship between the (crucial) business activities, their activities, and the KPI results. However, the managers from the CS department were less involved in the project because their department head gave them less leeway during the development stage. He had his doubts: "We tend to measure for measurement sake, instead of measuring for managing sake." This resulted in a KPI set that did not completely represent managers responsibility areas.

The conclusion was that the final score for the development stage at EIS was a +, which indicates that most of the behavioral factors for this stage were satisfied.

Use stage.   Managers from the FA department had a positive attitude toward the use of the performance management system because they viewed the KPIs as important for their own functioning, especially in managing their staff. Their indicators matched their responsibility areas well. The managers frequently made analyses that, however, hardly led to actions being reported in the management report. The FA indicator set was regularly evaluated and updated. The new CSF/KPI report was a real living instrument in the FA department.

Managers in the CS department, and especially the head of the department, seemed to have made less use of the performance management system: The CS KPIs were not actively discussed and evaluated. The number of indicators used decreased significantly in relation to the starting set of KPIs. The KPI set was not regularly evaluated or updated, making the indicators decreasingly relevant for CS managers. Since June 1996, only four procurement KPIs were reported. The department head saw targets as speculative and, therefore, no actions were taken on lagging actuals. CS managers saw the KPI set as a snapshot at a point in time. The manager of F&P commented: "KPIs should be a tool that is important to run your business, but it is not seen that way at CS. The FA department head manages the people in a straightforward manner and she introduced the KPIs when this was deemed necessary. The CS department head is not as performance-focused in all aspects. For example, he sets targets for the KPIs but then does not monitor the results. In his department, people were less enthusiastic and showed less commitment. With hindsight, I should have been more involved during the development of KPIs at CS and also in embedding these into the department."

In general, the CSF/KPI report got less priority in both departments due to the rather noncommittal manner in which the report was used for managing the departments. Managers were hardly held accountable by the F&P manager for their KPI results, and no linkage existed between the reward system and the results of the KPIs. Managers often said they had no time for reporting or taking actions, and frequently these excuses were simply accepted. If a turbulent working situation existed, the people tended to see the CSF/KPI report not as a number one priority. If managers were occasionally held accountable for their results, it was sometimes felt as a threat: I felt that a blaming culture existed at EIS, as an FA staff member agreed: "There exists a real blame culture within EIS. Managers specifically look at how good or bad you perform, they do not look at the causes for this performance."

The conclusion was that the final score for the use stage at EIS was a + for the FA department, which indicates that the behavioral factors for this stage were satisfied at this department, and a − for the CS department, indicating that the behavioral factors for this stage were not satisfied at this department.

Exhibit 3.14 gives the scores for the behavioral factors in the starting, development, and use stages. For each stage the final score is also given.

Exhibit 3.14 **Behavioral Factors Scores for the Starting, Development, and Use Stages at EIS**

Behavioral Factor	Analysis	FA	CS
Starting Stage			
Managers accept the need for performance management.	There was a positive attitude at the start of the CSF/KPI project. Managers wanted to employ the performance indicators to monitor where the organization stood (especially after the financial control project) and where the organization wanted to go with regard to external and internal performance.	+	+
Managers have earlier (positive) experiences with performance management.	All managers had positive previous experiences with performance measurement, which created a positive attitude at the start of the CSF/KPI project.	+	+
Managers agree on the starting time.	There was a clear and unambiguous starting time of the project. Managers saw the CSF/KPI project as a logical next step after the control project.	+	+

Exhibit 3.14 **Continued**

Behavioral Factor	Analysis	FA	CS
Starting Stage (continued)			
Managers have been involved in decision making around the project start time.	The managers were closely involved in the decision-making process.	+	+
Managers work in a stable, relatively tranquil environment.	Managers were, in their opinion, not able to spend enough time on the CSF/KPI project. The project team had to perform most of the activities. This was caused because the organization at that time had to install a number of changes in the business processes (for example, the still ongoing control project and the procurement model project).	0	0
Final score *starting* stage		+	+
Development Stage			
Managers have an active role during the development stage of the performance management system project.	Managers were highly involved in the discussions and workshops about the CSFs and KPIs to be developed.	+	+
Managers are informed about the status of the performance management system project.	Managers were frequently informed about the project status, by means of workshops and meetings.	+	+
Managers understand the meaning of KPIs.	The managers were familiar with the short definitions in the management report, but were not always familiar with the long definitions in a definition document.	+	+
Managers are involved in defining KPIs.	Managers were highly involved in the development of the KPI definitions.	+	+
Managers have insight into the relationship between business processes and CSFs/KPIs.	KPIs were defined for the (crucial) business activities of the departments. A clear relationship between KPIs and the (crucial) business activities of the departments existed.	+	+
Managers are involved in setting KPI targets.	For each performance indicator, a target was set in the management report. Managers were actively involved in the determination of targets.	+	+

(continues)

Exhibit 3.14   **Continued**

Behavioral Factor	*Analysis*	*FA*	*CS*
Development Stage (continued)			
Managers are involved in making the CSF/KPI/BSC report layout.	Managers were actively involved in the set up of the content and layout of the management report.	+	+
Managers understand the CSF/KPI/BSC reporting.	The finance and procurement reports were comprehensible to the managers. Colors, graphics, tables, and standard formats characterized the management report.	+	+
Managers can influence the KPIs assigned to them.	Managers felt responsible for the performance indicators which referred to the department and which they could influence themselves.	+	+
Managers accept the promoter.	Managers accepted the manager F&P as promoter of the project.	+	+
Managers find the performance management system relevant because it has a clear internal control purpose.	The management report was developed from an internal point of view.	+	+
Managers find the performance management system relevant because only those stakeholders' interests are incorporated that are important to the organization's success.	The management report was developed from an internal point of view. The service managers of EIS and the IT managers of the customers of EIS did not have influence on the content of the management report.	+	+
Managers use the CSFs/KPIs/BSC that match their responsibility areas.	For the FA and CS departments, different sets of CSFs and KPIs were developed. In general, the finance indicators gave a clear picture of the responsibility area of the manager. The procurement indicators were less successful in giving this view.	+	−
Managers have insight into the relationship between strategy and CSFs/KPIs.	CSFs and KPIs were, as described in the definition document, derived from the strategy of EIS. However, managers did not make use of this working document, and therefore, the relationship between the CSFs and KPIs and the strategy was hardly	−	−

Exhibit 3.14 **Continued**

Behavioral Factor	*Analysis*	*FA*	*CS*
Development Stage (continued)			
	recognized. Apart from that, there was no real clear relationship described in the definition document.		
Managers see that the promoter spends enough time on the performance management system implementation.	The sponsor spent little time on the CSF/KPI project: about 3 days of the total of 50 working days on the CSF/KPI project. This was done on purpose as the sponsor was of the opinion that the managers themselves should spend most of the time.	–	–
Managers' information processing capabilities are not exceeded by the number of CSFs/KPIs.	There was insufficient data to be able to judge this.	NA	NA
Managers' KPI sets are aligned with their responsibility areas.	There was insufficient data to be able to judge this.	NA	NA
Managers are actively communicating about the performance management system project.	There was insufficient data to be able to judge this.	NA	NA
Final score *development* stage		+	+
Use Stage			
Managers do not experience CSFs/KPIs/BSC as threatening.	The managers did not experience the results on KPIs as a threat.	+	+
Managers realize the importance of CSFs/KPIs/BSC to their performance.	The use of CSFs and KPIs turned out to be important for the control of the business processes and for a structured way of showing where improvements were needed.	+	+
Managers have sole responsibility for a KPI.	For each KPI, a single manager was responsible, although the results of certain indicators could be influenced by more than one person.	+	+

(continues)

Exhibit 3.14 **Continued**

Behavioral Factor	Analysis	FA	CS
Use Stage (continued)			
Managers can use their CSFs/KPIs/BSC for managing their employees.	FA managers, and to a lesser degree CS managers, saw as advantages of performance measurement: the use of KPIs as a tool for structuring discussions; and the way to get a clear picture of what happened inside the department and where the department wanted to go.	+	0
Managers' results on CSFs/KPIs/BSC are openly communicated.	The openness about the results of performance indicators was high. Some results of performance indicators were placed on a bulletin board in the hall. However, the CS department head communicated less information than the FA department head.	+	0
Managers agree on changes in the CSF/KPI set.	Inside the unit, consensus existed about changes with regard to the FA indicators. No changes took place in the CS indicators because these were hardly looked at by department head and managers.	+	−
Managers trust the performance information.	In general, the FA management report was considered to be reliable. Few discussions about the reliability took place. The KPI report of CS was hardly used and only limited attention was paid to the reliability.	+	−
Managers are involved in making analyses.	FA managers frequently made analyses. These analyses were put in the FA management report. CS managers did not make analyses.	+	−
Managers clearly see the promoter using the performance management system.	The sponsor talked about the indicators with the FA managers, but it was not clear what the quality of these conversations was. The sponsor could not speak to the CS managers about the KPIs because they hardly used their KPIs.	+	−
Managers have enough time to work with their CSFs/KPIs/BSC.	Managers seemed not to have enough time to do their daily activities. As a result, and also because some KPIs were hardly used for the managing of daily activities at both departments, the time spent on KPIs was limited.	0	0

Exhibit 3.14 **Continued**

Behavioral Factor	Analysis	FA	CS
Use Stage (continued)			
Managers' frames of reference contain similar KPIs.	For some KPIs of FA, the results were compared with other EIS sites. This was difficult because the procedures and systems of sites differed. No structured comparison took place for the indicators of CS.	0	–
Managers trust good-quality analyses.	The analysis for FA was described at a high level. In general, these analyses were open, but not very specific. There were no analyses made at CS.	0	–
Managers are stimulated to improve their performance.	At EIS, managers rather quickly blamed others for their mistakes (blame culture). This was especially visible in the CS department.	0	–
Managers' activities are supported by KPIs.	FA managers formulated actions for their indicators, but these actions were not documented in the management report. CS managers hardly formulated actions for their indicators.	0	–
Managers have insight into the relationship between KPIs and financial results.	The actions and financial consequences of actions were not mentioned in the management report. Consequently, there was no insight into the relationship between KPIs and financial results.	–	–
Managers have insight into the relationship between cause and effect.	At both departments, no explicit cause and effect relationships were identified.	–	–
Managers are involved in forecasting.	Forecasts for KPIs were infrequently made.	–	–
Managers use the performance management system regularly during the planning and control cycle.	Managers were not held accountable for the results of the KPIs on a regular basis. The use of KPIs seemed rather noncommittal.	–	–
Managers' use of the performance management system is stimulated by the reward structure.	The managers were assessed on their tasks and goals but not on the results of their KPIs. There was no link between KPI results and the reward structure.	–	–

(continues)

Exhibit 3.14   **Continued**

Behavioral Factor	Analysis	FA	CS
Use Stage (continued)			
Managers and their controlling systems have a mutual trust.	There was insufficient data to be able to judge this.	NA	NA
Managers do not get discouraged by the collection of performance data.	There was insufficient data to be able to judge this.	NA	NA
Managers find the performance management system relevant due to regular evaluations.	There was insufficient data to be able to judge this.	NA	NA
Managers trust good-quality forecasts.	There was insufficient data to be able to judge this.	NA	NA
Final score *use* stage		+	−

Criteria for regular use.   Exhibit 3.15 gives the scores for the criteria for regular use, which indicate whether the implementation of the CSFs and KPIs at the two departments of EIS can be considered to be successful.

The use of the CSFs and KPIs in the F&P unit could not be called an unqualified success: A clear difference in use of the indicators between departments FA and CS was found. In the FA department, the use of and the communication about the KPI report was frequent and increased in time. Changes in the CSF/KPI set were regularly made (changes in definitions and targets, and adding and skipping of indicators). There was one point of attention, however. The FA department head, who recognized the importance of the indicators and was continuously busy with reviewing and updating the CSF/KPI set, would leave EIS in June 1997. Consequently, a real danger existed in that the CSF/KPI report of FA could receive less attention in the future.

In the CS department, the use of and the communication about the KPI report was irregular and clearly decreased after the initial introduction. The procurement report was, during the time of the case study research, generated only on an ad hoc basis. Of the 17 procurement indicators that were originally developed, only four indicators were still in use. Recently, the department experienced some organizational problems, which resulted in the CSF/KPI report's receiving even less attention. The head of CS used the report not (anymore) as a tool for control

Exhibit 3.15 **Criteria for Regular Use Scores for EIS**

Criteria for Regular Use	Analysis	FA	CS
CSFs, KPIs, and BSC incorporated in the regular management reporting	The CSFs and KPIs were an integral part of the regular management reporting. However, the CS report only contained a limited number of KPIs.	+	0
Increased performance management system use by managers	The use of indicators at the FA department increased in time. The use of the indicators at the CS department decreased in time.	+	−
Regular communication about KPI results	Communication between the manager F&P and the FA department about its indicators regularly took place. The communication with the CS department took place infrequently and ad hoc.	+	−
Plans for follow-up projects	There were no formal plans for the continuation of the CSF/KPI project.	−	−
Difference in attitude toward performance management, between project start and currently	In both departments, there initially was a positive attitude toward performance management. At FA, the managers still were positive; however, at CS the initial enthusiasm had considerably decreased.	+	0
Organizational results improved, through the performance management system use	It seemed the performance of the unit stayed constant.	0	0
Organizational results improved, objectively	It seemed the results of FA were improving, and those of CS were decreasing. It was not clear whether this was through performance management system use or through other factors (like personnel problems at CS).	0	−
Final score criteria for regular use		+	−

but more as an information tool for the accountability toward his customers. He could explain some of the difficulties customers experienced with CS with information from the KPI report.

A general point of attention was that the finance and the procurement management reports were not an integral part of the planning and control cycle in the unit. The managers from the unit were not really held accountable for the results of the KPIs. In addition to this, the management report was hardly used for formulating and undertaking actions by both the FA and CS heads and the manager F&P. The danger existed in that the management report would increasingly be used for, as one manager put it, "measuring to know, instead of measuring to manage." The conclusion was that the final score for the criteria for regular use at EIS was a + for the FA department, which indicates that the implementation of the CSFs and KPIs was a success at that department. The final score for the CS department was a −, which indicates that the implementation of the CSFs and KPIs was a failure at that department. This analysis was discussed with the manager of F&P, who shared my opinion. According to him, the performance management system was hardly used in the CS department, while at the same time the FA department used it extensively.

ANALYSIS OF CASE STUDIES

In this section, the two questions are investigated by applying pattern matching, which allows patterns to be discerned between the various scores of the cases. These patterns tell us which behavioral factors, theoretically predicted to be important, coincide with the criteria for regular use. Pattern matching is applied to identify patterns between the scores on the individual behavioral factors and the criteria for regular use, and between the end scores for the three stages and the scores for the criteria for regular use. The assumption in pattern matching is that the behavioral factors are independent. This is why the factors have not been weighed. For pattern matching, a complete match between the scores of all cases gives a complete coincidence, indicating that these behavioral factors seem to have a general similarity with a successful implementation and use of a performance management system. These behavioral factors can consequently be considered to be essential. A match between two or three scores gives a partial coincidence, indicating these behavioral factors have a partial similarity with the criteria for regular use. These behavioral factors may be important to the successful implementation and use of a performance management system. Finally, a match between none or one of the scores indicates there is no coincidence, meaning these behavioral factors may not be important to the successful implementation and use of a performance management system.

As an example, we look at some of the behavioral factors in the use stage. The scores for four factors (U1, U9, U13, and U15) are compared with the scores for the criteria for regular use. These scores have been transferred into Exhibit 3.16 from the four case studies as described in

Exhibit 3.16   **Pattern Matching Example**

No.	Behavioral Factor	AZU	EIS-FA	EIS-CS	Kad.	Importance
U1	Managers have insight into the relationship between KPIs and financial results.	–	–	–	0	No
U9	Managers are involved in making analyses.	0	+	–	+	Yes
U13	Managers realize the importance of CSFs/KPIs/BSC to their performances.	0	+	+	+	Partial
U15	Managers can use their CSFs/KPIs/BSC for managing their employees.	+	+	0	+	Partial
Final score criteria for regular use		**0**	**+**	**–**	**+**	

the previous sections.[3] If we look at factor U9, a complete match of the four scores is found (score 0 + – + of U9 corresponds with the final score 0 + – + of the criteria for regular use). Behavioral factors U13 and U15 have three respectively two matches with the final score of the criteria for regular use and, therefore, partially coincide. Behavioral factor U1 has only one coinciding score and is, therefore, deemed to be of no importance to the successful implementation and use of a performance management system.

Pattern Matching of the Behavioral Factors

To answer the first question *(Which behavioral factors—listed in Exhibit 2.4—contribute to the successful implementation and use of a performance management system?)*, pattern matching is applied to identify patterns between the scores on the individual behavioral factors found in all the cases and all the scores for the criteria for regular use. Exhibit 3.17 gives the results of this pattern matching. Area A lists the behavioral factors. Area B gives the scores from the case studies. Area C lists the results of the pattern matching between the behavioral factors and the final score (column "Imp." for Important) and the subscores (columns 1–7) of the criteria for regular use. The detailed scores are given in the second table. Complete and partial matches between the behavioral factors and the criteria have been given a dark shade. A complete match is also denoted with a C. In area B the behavioral factor(s) that prevented a complete

Exhibit 3.17 **Results of Pattern Matching Between the Behavioral Factors and the Criteria for Regular Use Scores for All the Case Studies**

A.		B.				C. Criteria for Regular Use							
No.	Behavioral Factor	AZU	EIS-FA	EIS-CS	Kad.	Imp.	1	2	3	4	5	6	7
Starting Stage													
S1	Managers accept the need for performance management.	+	+	+	+						■	■	■
S2	Managers agree on the starting time.	0	+	+	+	■			■		■	■	■
S3	Managers have been involved in decision making about the project start time.	−	+	+	−								
S4	Managers have earlier (positive) experiences with performance management.	+	+	+	+	■			■		■	■	■
S5	Managers work in a stable, relatively tranquil environment.	−	0	0	0		■	■					
Development Stage													
D1	Managers have an active role during the development stage of the performance management system project.	−	+	+	−								
D2	Managers are informed about the status of the performance management system project.	NA	+	+	−								

D3	Managers are actively communicating about the performance management system project.	NA	+	+	–
D4	Managers understand the meaning of KPIs.	0	+	+	NA
D5	Managers are involved in defining KPIs.	–	+	+	–
D6	Managers have insight into the relationship between strategy and CSFs/KPIs.	–	–	–	0
D7	Managers have insight into the relationship between business processes and CSFs/KPIs.	0	+	+	0
D8	Managers are involved in setting KPI targets.	–	+	+	0
D9	Managers' KPI sets are aligned with their responsibility areas.	–	+	–	0
D10	Managers are involved in making the CSF/KPI/BSC report layout.	–	+	+	–
D11	Managers understand the CSF/KPI/BSC reporting.	+	+	+	0
D12	Managers use the CSFs/KPIs/BSC that match their responsibility areas.	NA	NA	NA	0

(continues)

Exhibit 3.17 Continued

	A.		B.				C. Criteria for Regular Use							
No.	Behavioral Factor	AZU	EIS-FA	EIS-CS	Kad.	Imp.	1	2	3	4	5	6	7
Development Stage (continued)													
D13	Managers can influence the KPIs assigned to them.	0	+	+	NA	▪			▪		▪	▪	
D14	Managers accept the promoter.	–	+	+	0								
D15	Managers see that the promoter spends enough time on the performance management system implementation.	NA	–	–	0					▪			
D16	Managers find the performance management system relevant because it has a clear internal control purpose.	+	+	+	+	▪			▪	▪	▪	▪	▪
D17	Managers find the performance management system relevant because only those stakeholders' interests are incorporated that are important to the organization's success.	NA	+	+	+	▪			▪		▪	▪	▪
Use Stage													
U1	Managers have insight into the relationship between KPIs and financial results.	–	–	–	0					▪			

124

U2	Managers do not get discouraged by the collection of performance data.	+	NA	NA	+
U3	Managers have insight into the relationship between cause and effect.	–	–	–	–
U4	Managers are involved in forecasting.	–	–	–	–
U5	Managers trust good-quality forecasts.	NA	NA	NA	NA
U6	Managers' activities are supported by KPIs.	NA	0	–	0
U7	Managers' frames of reference contain similar KPIs.	–	0	–	+
U8	Managers trust the performance information.	0	+	–	0
U9	Managers are involved in making analyses.	0	+	+	+
U10	Managers trust good-quality analyses.	0	0	–	0
U11	Managers' information processing capabilities are not exceeded by the number of CSFs/KPIs.	–	NA	NA	–
U12	Managers have enough time to work with their CSFs/KPIs/BSC.	+	0	0	+
U13	Managers realize the importance of CSFs/KPIs/BSC to their performance.	0	+	+	+

(continues)

Exhibit 3.17 Continued

	A.		B.				C. Criteria for Regular Use							
No.	Behavioral Factor	AZU	EIS-FA	EIS-CS	Kad.	Imp.	1	2	3	4	5	6	7
Use Stage (continued)													
U14	Managers do not experience CSFs/KPIs/BSC as threatening.	+	+	+	+	■			■		■	■	■
U15	Managers can use their CSFs/KPIs/BSC for managing their employees.	+	+	0	+						■	■	C
U16	Managers have sole responsibility for a KPI.	–	+	+	0								
U17	Managers clearly see the promoter using the performance management system.	–	+	–	0	■				■		■	
U18	Managers and their controlling systems have a mutual trust.	NA	NA	NA	+								
U19	Managers find the performance management system relevant due to regular evaluations.	–	NA	NA	–								
U20	Managers use the performance management system regularly during the planning and control cycle.	0	NA	NA	–								
U21	Managers agree on changes in the CSF/KPI set.	–	+	–	–	■	■		■			■	
U22	Managers are stimulated to improve their performance.	NA	0	–	+								

126

	+	+	0	+							C
U23 Managers' results on CSFs/KPIs/BSC are openly communicated.											
U24 Managers' use of the performance management system is stimulated by the reward structure.	-	-	-	-							
Number of shaded areas:	9	2	11	5	18	6	6	18	12	15	17	12

No.	Criteria for Regular Use	AZU	EIS-FA	EIS-CA	Kad.
1	Organizational results improved, through the performance management system use	-	0	0	+
2	Organizational results improved, objectively	0	0	0	0
3	Increased performance management system use by managers	0	+	-	+
4	Plans for follow-up projects	+	-	-	0
5	Difference in attitude toward performance management, between project start and currently	0	+	0	+
6	Regular communication about KPI results	0	+	-	+
7	CSFs, KPIs, and BSC incorporated in the regular management reporting	+	+	0	+
Imp.	**Final score criteria for regular use**	0	+	-	+

matching with the final score for the criteria for regular use (denoted by a dark shade in the Imp. column) has been given a light shade.

Based on the results of pattern matching, the first question *(Which behavioral factors—listed in Exhibit 2.4—contribute to the successful implementation and use of a performance management system?)*, can be answered in the following way: Eighteen of the behavioral factors, derived from the behavioral factors in the literature, seem to be important to the successful implementation and use of a performance management system.

Pattern Matching of the Stages

To answer the second question *(Are behavioral factors from the starting and development stages more important to the successful implementation and use of a performance management system than those of the use stage?)*, pattern matching is applied to identify patterns between the end scores of the stages and the final scores of the criteria for regular use. Pattern matching is performed in a similar manner as in the previous section. If a complete or partial match is found for a particular stage, it is deemed that this stage must be executed properly in order to obtain a regularly used performance management system. Exhibit 3.18 gives the results of pattern matching for the starting, development, and use stages.

The scores for the use stage coincide completely with the final scores for the criteria for regular use. In other words, it seems there is a relation between a well-executed use stage and a good final score. The scores for the starting and development stages, however, coincide partially or not at all with the scores for the criteria for regular use. This tells us that there is no relationship between how well these stages have been executed and the final score. So, even a well-executed starting and/or development stage is no guarantee for a good final score, that is, a regularly used performance management system. Consequently, the result for the second question *(Are behavioral factors from the starting and development stages*

Exhibit 3.18 **Final Scores for All the Stages and All the Case Studies**

Stage	AZU	EIS-FA	EIS-CS	Kad.	Important
Starting	0	+	+	+	Partial
Development	–	+	+	0	No
Use	0	+	–	+	Yes
Final score criteria for regular use	0	+	–	+	

more important to the successful implementation and use of a performance management system than those of the use stage?) is negative.

Discussion of the Results

The results of the pattern matching indicate that there are 18 behavioral factors that coincide with the final score for the criteria for regular use. The result that 10 of these 18 factors are from the use stage matches the result found from pattern matching the stages. There, the use stage turned out to best coincide with the criteria for regular use (see previous section). It is possible to group the 18 important behavioral factors from Exhibit 3.17 together in categories in such a way that an overview appears of the areas an organization has to pay special attention to increase the chance of implementing a new performance management system that will be regularly used (Exhibit 3.19).

Exhibit 3.19 **Overview of the Behavioral Factors, Important to the Implementation of a Regularly Used Performance Management System**

Classification Scheme Part	Areas of Attention, to Obtain a Regularly Used Performance Management System	Behavioral Factors
Performance management system	Managers' understanding— *A good understanding by managers of the nature of performance management*	• D4. Managers understand the meaning of KPIs. • D7. Managers have insight into the relationship between business processes and CSFs/KPIs. • U7. Managers' frames of reference contain similar KPIs. • U21. Managers agree on changes in the CSF/KPI set.
Controlled system	Managers' attitude—*A positive attitude of managers toward performance management, performance management system, and the project*	• S2. Managers agree on the starting time. • S4. Managers have earlier (positive) experiences with performance management. • U13. Managers realize the importance of CSFs/KPIs/BSC to their performance. • U14. Managers do not experience CSFs/KPIs/BSC as threatening.

(continues)

Exhibit 3.19 **Continued**

Classification Scheme Part	Areas of Attention, to Obtain a Regularly Used Performance Management System	Behavioral Factors
Controlling system	Performance management system alignment—*A good match between managers' responsibilities and the performance management system*	■ D9. Managers' KPI sets are aligned with their responsibility areas. ■ D13. Managers can influence the KPIs assigned to them. ■ U9. Managers are involved in making analyses. ■ U15. Managers can use their CSFs/KPIs/BSC for managing their employees.
Internal environment	Organizational culture—*An organizational culture focused on using the performance management system to improve*	■ U23. Managers' results on CSFs/ KPIs/BSC are openly communicated. ■ U22. Managers are stimulated to improve their performance. ■ U8. Managers trust the performance information. ■ U17. Managers clearly see the promoter using the performance management system.
External environment	Performance management system focus—*A clear focus of the performance management system on internal management and control*	■ D16. Managers find the performance management system relevant because it has a clear internal control purpose. ■ D17. Managers find the performance management system relevant because only those stakeholders' interests are incorporated that are important to the organization's success.

It is also possible to group the least important behavioral factors together in categories in such a way that an overview appears of the areas an organization does not have to pay special attention to during the implementation of a new performance management system. For this, the behavioral factors that do not have a single match in Exhibit 3.17 are grouped together. If a factor had "N/A" two or more times, it was not included in a category (Exhibit 3.20).

Exhibit 3.20 **Overview of the Behavioral Factors, Least Important to the Implementation of a Regularly Used Performance Management System**

Classification Scheme Part	Areas of Least Attention, to Obtain a Regularly Used Performance Management System	Behavioral Factors
Performance management system	Managers' involvement— *Direct involvement of managers in developing the new performance management system*	▪ S3. Managers have been involved in decision making around the project start time. ▪ D1. Managers have an active role during the development stage of the performance management system project. ▪ D2. Managers are informed about the status of the performance management system project. ▪ D3. Managers are actively communicating about the performance management system project. ▪ D5. Managers are involved in defining KPIs. ▪ D8. Managers are involved in setting KPI targets. ▪ D10. Managers are involved in making the CSF/KPI/BSC report layout. ▪ D11. Managers understand the CSF/KPI/BSC reporting.
Controlled system	–	
Controlling system		▪ D14. Managers accept the promoter. ▪ U16. Managers have sole responsibility for a KPI.
Internal environment	–	
External environment	–	

As expected, because no relationship was found between this stage and the criteria for regular use, most behavioral factors that are least important belong to the development stage (D). It seems an organization does not necessarily have to actively involve managers in the development of the KPIs and the balanced scorecard (BSC) to obtain a regularly used performance management system. This matches the observation that in many of the projects I have participated in, a special project group performed the development activities, after which the future users of the performance management system (the managers) evaluated and approved the developed KPIs and BSC.

An interesting anomaly shows up in Exhibit 3.18. While the comparable departments EIS-FA and EIS-CS have equal scores for the starting and development stages, the scores for the use stage are diametrically opposed. In Exhibit 3.17, the scores for EIS-CS prevent a complete coincidence between behavioral factor scores and criteria for regular use scores 11 times (i.e., 11 lightly shaded areas in the exhibit). How can this be explained? In both departments, a similar favorable starting situation existed. In both departments, the same approach for the development of the performance management system was used and a representative set of CSFs and KPIs was made. Only in relation to the use of the performance management system did both departments differ dramatically. This difference seemed to be caused by the attitude of the department heads toward management control and the resulting management styles they used to control their departments. The head of FA had a stricter and more structured control over the department and used the CSFs and KPIs as an extra support for getting information about the status and performance of the department. The head of CS used a looser and less structured control over the department; the head was less interested in the performance management system and regarded the CSF/KPI report as not providing enough value for this type of control.

If the AZU scores in Exhibit 3.17 are examined, it becomes apparent that nine times the score prevents a complete coincidence, which means in nine instances the score for a behavioral factor deviates from the final score (i.e., the average score for all the cases examined). This suggests that at AZU there may be additional factors that may be important to the successful implementation and use of a performance management system. A closer look into that case study reveals that the difference in frequency of performance management system use can possibly be explained by the difference in conception of the two categories of managers at AZU (medical and administrative) in regard to a performance management system. In Exhibit 3.17, more evidence that other factors may be involved can be found. In area C of this exhibit, the most darkly shaded areas can be found for regular use criteria 3 (increased performance management system use by managers) and 6 (regular communication about KPI results). These criteria are concerned with managers regularly using a performance management system for a specific type of use (in this case, communication).

Taking all these findings together gives an indication that there may be more factors involved in play that are important to the successful implementation and use of a performance management system than discussed in this thesis so far. Two recent studies into the behavioral aspects of performance management systems implementation and performance management systems use can shed some light on the nature of these factors. The first study[4] found that managers' cognitive limitations may prevent organizations to fully benefit from a performance management system, and that cognitive differences between managers may lead them to use the performance management system differently. If Exhibit 3.19 is examined in the light of these findings, it is conspicuous that two of the five areas of attention could be related to the cognitive and interpersonal abilities of a manager (managers' understanding and managers' attitude). The second study[5] found that positive outcomes from performance management system use were mostly determined by the effectiveness by which it is used as a management control device (defined in terms of effective measurement, comprehensive performance, and weight of the measurement dimensions), while these outcomes were not attributable to its use as a communication device. Positive outcomes are generated by a better strategic alignment of employees and a better motivation, indicating the existence of causal relations between performance management system design, management control use, managerial and employee behavior, and performance. Although these findings contradict some of the findings displayed in Exhibit 3.17, they are still an indication that the type of performance management system use may be important for the success of that performance management system.

As the aspects of cognitive and interpersonal abilities of managers and types of performance management system use were not explicitly taken into account during the investigation described in Part One of this book, and because I had an inclination they could be essential in answering the questions of this investigation more satisfactory, I decided to start a second investigation. In this investigation, I tried to relate performance management system use and organizational performance to management styles. Individual managers have distinctive ways of processing information and making decisions, which can be captured in various management styles. These styles then result in different ways of utilizing accounting and information systems, so that using any particular system depends on the style of the user. Management styles are composed of the cognitive and interpersonal abilities of managers and express themselves in individual competencies and observable behaviors of managers. In this respect, a competence is a feature of an individual that has a causal relationship with effective and/or excellent behavior at performing a certain task or in a certain situation. Management styles are considered one of the important and permanent drivers of managerial behavior. Developers and users of performance management systems should take these management styles into account when they develop and implement a new performance management system. The second investigation focused strictly on observable behavior: How do managers behave when they use a performance management system and how do managers behave when they manage (management styles). *Why* managers behave or do not behave in a certain way is *not* part of this investigation. This would require further in-depth psychological research, which lays beyond the scope of this book. The objective of the second investigation is to find answers to the questions: *Which management styles are related to which types of performance management system use?* and *Do specific management styles and types of performance management system use have an effect on organizational performance?* The results of this investigation are described in Part Two of this book.

ENDNOTES

1. At the organization's request, the company name has been changed.
2. Ibid.
3. For the analysis, the EIS case has been separated into two cases, EIS-FA and EIS-CS, giving a total of four case studies.
4. Lipe, M. G., and S. E. Salterio (2000). "The balanced scorecard: Judgmental effects of common and unique performance measures." *Accounting Review* 75, 3:283–298.
5. Malina, M. A., and F. M. Selto (2000). *Communicating and controlling strategy: An empirical study of the effectiveness of the balanced scorecard.* Paper presented at the AAA Annual Conference, Philadelphia, August 13–16.

Part Two

MANAGEMENT STYLES

4

RELATIONSHIP BETWEEN PERFORMANCE MANAGEMENT SYSTEM USES AND MANAGEMENT STYLES

In Chapter 3, a description was given of the case-study research performed to investigate the importance of various behavioral factors for the successful implementation and use of a performance management system. This chapter describes the specific management styles that managers theoretically should display to make frequent, day-to-day use of a performance management system for specific purposes. To identify which management styles have an influence on the use of a performance management system, the possible uses of a performance management system are identified first and after that the management styles that theoretically have to be present for managers to become a regular user of a performance management system are identified. The so-called performance management system use factors and management style factors are operationalized in a questionnaire. Assumptions are drafted about the relations between the identified performance management system use factors and management style factors and validated, using the questionnaire at 11 organizations.

PERFORMANCE MANAGEMENT SYSTEM USES

According to the literature described in Chapter 1, managers use a performance management system which includes critical success factors (CSFs), key performance indicators (KPIs), and the balanced scorecard (BSC) to obtain better quality information, timelier information, better support for their activities, better communication, and an aligned culture. To determine if managers are indeed using the performance management system in their organization for these purposes, a questionnaire that measures specific system uses is required. In the field of management information systems (MIS), much research has been done into the use of information systems and the choice of suitable variables to measure it. Due to the similarity between a performance management system and an MIS in general, an MIS questionnaire was used to measure the use of a performance management system. To this end, the "measures of system use" questionnaire of Doll and Torkzadeh was selected because this questionnaire seemed to fit well with the behavioral patterns described in the previous chapters.[1] Doll and Torkzadeh measure the use of an MIS along several dimensions of system use of an MIS. *System use* is defined as the various applications for which an MIS can be used. An MIS is defined as a system in an organization that uses information technology (IT) to provide information and communication services.[2] Doll and Torkzadeh's questionnaire does not investigate how often or how long an MIS is used by respondents. Rather, the questionnaire asks respondents for which purpose(s) they use an MIS. Each specific purpose of MIS use matches a dimension of system use. An example of such a purpose is: "I use the MIS to help me explain my decisions." In total, the Doll and Torkzadeh questionnaire contains 30 purposes, which are categorized in three dimensions of system use (Exhibit 4.1).

A performance management system can be regarded as a type of MIS because it is an integral part of the planning and control cycle of an organization and provides the manager with information about this cycle. Comparison between the system use given in Exhibit 4.1 and the performance management system use mentioned at the start of this section shows that there is a correspondence between the two. For decision support, better quality information and timelier information is needed, which can be provided by a performance management system. Work integration results in better support of management and in an aligned culture. Finally, to improve customer service, better communication is needed, which can be supported by a performance management system. This correspondence increases the confidence in assuming that the Doll and Torkzadeh questionnaire can be applied to measure the various types of use a manager actually makes of a performance management system. This assumption has to be verified before commencing with testing assumptions. To this end, the questionnaire has been adapted to fit the research into the use of a performance management system. Before sending out the adapted questionnaire to the case study companies, it was discussed with some of my colleagues. This resulted in further adaptation of

Exhibit 4.1   **System Use and MIS Use Factors, According to Doll and Torkzadeh (1998)**

System Use	*MIS Use Factor*	*Definition*
Decision support	Problem solving	The extent that an MIS is used to analyze cause-and-effect relationships (such as to make sense out of the data)
	Decision rationalization	The extent that an MIS is used to improve the decision-making processes or explain/justify the reasons for decisions
Work integration	Horizontal integration	The extent that an MIS is used to coordinate work activities with others in one's work group
	Vertical integration	The extent that an MIS is used to plan one's own work, monitor performance, and communicate vertically to coordinate one's work with superiors and subordinates
Customer service	Customer service	The extent that an MIS is used to service internal and/or external customers

the list, by excluding 8 of the 30 measures of use. Exhibit 4.2 lists for each performance management system use (for instance, decision rationalization) the related measures of use (such as "I use the performance management system to help me explain my decisions").

Exhibit 4.2   **Questionnaire on Measures of Performance Management System Use[a]**

Decision Rationalization

R1   I use the performance management system to help me explain my decisions.

R2   I use the performance management system to help me justify my decisions.

R3   I use the performance management system to help me make explicit the reasons for my decisions.

R6   I use the performance management system to improve the effectiveness and efficiency of the decision process.

R7   I use the performance management system to make the decision process more rational.

Problem Solving

P1   I use the performance management system to decide how best to approach a problem.

P4   I use the performance management system to check my thinking against the data.

(continues)

Exhibit 4.2 **Continued**

Problem Solving (continued)

P5   I use the performance management system to make sense out of the data.

P6   I use the performance management system to analyze why problems occur.

Horizontal Integration

H1   I use the performance management system to communicate with other people in my work group.

H2   My work group and I use the performance management system to coordinate our activities.

H3   I use the performance management system to coordinate activities with others in my work group.

Vertical Integration

V2   I use the performance management system to monitor my own performance.

V3   I use the performance management system to plan my work.

V4   I use the performance management system to communicate with people who report to me.

V5   I use the performance management system to communicate with people to whom I report.

V8   I use the performance management system to get feedback on job performance.

Customer Service

C1   I use the performance management system to deal more strategically with internal and/or external customers.

C2   I use the performance management system to serve internal and/or external customers.

C3   I use the performance management system to improve the quality of customer service.

C4   I use the performance management system to serve customers more creatively.

C5   I use the performance management system to exchange information with internal and/or external customers.

---

[a] Some numbers are missing because the original Doll questionnaire is longer than this adapted questionnaire. Compared to the original questionnaire, the measures of use P2, P3, R4, H4, V1, V6, and V7 were removed. For each performance management system use, at least three components were present.

Source: Adapted from Doll, W. J., and G. Torkzadeh (1998). "Developing a multidimensional measure of system use in an organizational context." *Information and Management* 33.

MANAGEMENT STYLES

To determine whether managers dispose of the management styles that are required for frequent, day-to-day use of a performance management system, I searched for a questionnaire that could investigate these styles. However, because no suitable questionnaire could be found, I constructed my own questionnaire based on the theoretical management styles and related behaviors found in the literature.

Thinking

If a person is capable of *analytical thinking,* he or she has the ability to identify cause-and-effect chains and relationships. He or she can understand a certain situation, subdivide this situation into various elements, and identify the causes and the effects step by step. Analytical thinking also means structuring the various aspects of a problem or situation, making comparisons systematically of these aspects, setting priorities on a rational basis, and identifying the causes of successive events, causal and if–then relationships. Managers behave in an analytical manner if they are able to use logical, rational processes to analyze and apply information; subdivide complex problems efficiently into various, workable elements; put elements into a logical causal order; use if–then reasoning to identify possible obstacles or to take decisions that will influence the future; and identify whether an approach is useful or not.

If a person is capable of *conceptual thinking,* he or she has the ability to understand a situation or a problem by gaining an overall view. Conceptual thinking comprises creative, conceptual, and inductive reasoning to implement existing concepts or define new concepts. Managers behave in a conceptual thinking manner if they are able to use abstract reasoning to make logical connections between different sources of information in order to gain an overall view of the problem and to translate complex information and insights into understandable, meaningful concepts.

Both analytical and conceptual thinking may be important to regular use of a performance management system because these are management styles that enable managers to gain insight into factors that influence the performance of the organization, as provided by the performance management system. Having these abilities at one's disposal means being able to analyze problems, generate solutions, and obtain improvements. In the planning stage, managers determine the targets for the KPIs. They can do this properly only if they have insight into the factors that are influencing these indicators and, therefore, which targets can be reached. In the control and measurement stages, managers compare the results of

KPIs with the targets, interpret variances, and look for causal relation-ships between the various results and KPIs. If they are able to explain unforeseen results, they can formulate actions to correct unfavorable vari-ances and identify improvement opportunities. All these activities require analytical and conceptual management styles.

Communication

If a person is capable of *communicating* effectively, he or she has the abil-ity to interact effectively with and convey information to other people. This includes the use of a range of communication methods, such as oral, written, graphical, and nonverbal communication. These methods are used both by sender and receiver of information. Managers behave in a communicative manner if they are able to listen objectively and repro-duce the content of a message in their own words; use different forms and styles of communication; speak effectively to individuals and groups of people; and express their needs, wishes, opinions and expectations to other people while taking people's feelings into consideration.

Effective communication may be important to regular use of a per-formance management system. In the planning stage, managers discuss the action plans with various groups of people and communicate the strategy, objectives, and actions to employees. In the measurement stage, managers must provide regular intermediate feedback on results to employees. And finally, in the feedback stage, managers discuss with other managers various issues that show up in the management reporting and possible corrective actions for these.

Cooperation

If a person is capable of *cooperation,* he or she has the ability to function as a member of a team in such a way that it makes execution of the team's activities easier. A team can be a group of people (a work team), a manage-ment team, or a department. This characteristic includes the genuine intention to cooperate with other people, to be part of a team, and to work together instead of individually or in competition with others. Managers behave in a teamwork and cooperative manner if they are able to motivate other team members to work on joint objectives; have insight into the strengths and weaknesses of other team members and use the strengths to further develop the team; cooperate in projects; share plans, information, and information sources with other team members; encourage a friendly, cooperative atmosphere in the team; detect and use opportunities to coop-erate; and share successes and responsibilities with the team.

Effective teamwork and cooperation may be important to regular use of a performance management system because the system cannot function without the willingness of people to cooperate. This willingness is closely related to the culture of an organization. To improve an organization and its processes, there has to be a culture of openness and trust. The attitude of constantly covering up problems will make the behavioral pattern of teamwork and cooperation meaningless. This will be a problem especially in the control stage, when managers have to signal and discuss problems and find solutions for these problems. Consequently, cooperation is essential to make these problems transparent in a safe environment. Teamwork and cooperation are also important in the planning and feedback stages, when employees need to be motivated to work together to achieve the targets that have been set.

Flexibility

If a person is capable of being flexible, he or she has the ability to adapt to the circumstances and particular environments he or she finds himself or herself in. This includes the ability to adapt oneself to and work in various situations and with various individuals and groups of persons. *Flexibility* and *adaptation* also include understanding and valuing different and opposing viewpoints to an issue, adjusting the chosen approach in case of changing circumstances, and adjusting or accepting changes in the organization or activities. Managers behave in a flexible and adaptive manner if they are able to adapt easily to various demands, changing priorities, and fast changes; are flexible in their view on issues; and adapt their approach in the light of changing circumstances.

Flexibility and adaptation may be important to regular use of a performance management system because these systems enhance continuous change. The organization tries to adjust itself quickly and efficiently to changes in the environment. An efficient and effective performance management system provides the information that not only often triggers these changes but is also needed to adapt to the changes. This requires managers to be open to differing viewpoints and consequently to be able to make fast and timely adjustments. This competence is especially relevant in the planning and control stages, in which the organization's current situation is closely examined and adaptations are made.

Behaviors Related to the Management Styles

Exhibit 4.3 lists for each management style its preferred behaviors. To avoid the possibility of managers giving socially desirable answers, behaviors have been formulated either in a positive or negative manner. The

Exhibit 4.3   **Management Styles and Behaviors Used in the Self-Constructed Questionnaire**

Analytical Thinking (AT)

—Uses logical and rational processes to analyze and apply information.

AT1   I take rational decisions even if my feelings tell me to take alternative ones.

AT2   My "intuition" and feelings guide the decisions that I finally make. (−)

—Efficiently divides complex problems into separate, workable elements.

AT3   When trying to understand a problem, I work it out to identify its different aspects.

—Puts things in a logical causal order.

AT4   When confronted with an unexpected outcome, I make a list of sequential events that might have caused it.

AT5   With many problems, I am not interested in what the causes were; they just have to be solved immediately! (−)

—Uses if–then reasoning to identify potential obstacles or to make decisions that will influence the future.

AT6   I try to predict the potential consequences and future courses of events resulting from implementation of alternative courses of action.

—Identifies whether an approach is useful and when it is not.

AT7   When facing a problem, I immediately make a decision, without first considering a number of possible alternatives. (−)

AT8   I consciously consider several different approaches before tackling a problem.

Conceptual Thinking (CT)

—Uses abstract reasoning to connect various sources of information logically.

CT1   I understand new things by seeing how they fit with what I already know.

CT2   When performing a task that is new to me, I first investigate how it is related to other tasks that I performed in the past.

—Identifies crucial information from various data and concepts.

CT3   I combine relevant information and concepts from several very different sources to get a clear picture of the situation.

CT4   When I need to assess a situation, I look at the information available. (−)

—Translates complex information and insights into understandable, meaningful concepts.

CT5   When I want to solve a complex problem, I try to redefine it into concepts that are recognizable to me.

CT6   I can get so intensively focused on specific details, that I forget the big picture. (−)

Exhibit 4.3 **Continued**

Communication (C)

—*Listens objectively and translates the content of the message in his or her own words.*

C1   I repeat something that someone says to me in my own words to ensure that I have understood the message correctly.

C2   When someone is speaking to me (or to an audience that I am part of), I am able to instantly stop thinking about anything else and concentrate on what is being said.

—*Uses various forms and styles of written communication.*

C3   I have a variety of writing styles from which I choose the most appropriate for the reader that I am addressing my correspondence to.

C4   I don't pay attention to the layout of my reports: It is the content that counts. (−)

—*Speaks effectively to individuals and groups of people.*

C5   After I have given a presentation, people ask me to give further clarifications. (−)

—*Expresses his or her needs, wishes, opinions, and expectations without hurting other people's feelings.*

C6   I pay particular attention to others' feelings when expressing myself.

C7   I only express my opinion or expectations when I expect people to accept them. (−)

Teamwork and Cooperation (TC)

—*Motivates team members to work toward shared targets.*

TC1   I encourage others in the group to work together.

—*Has insight into strengths and weaknesses of team members and uses the strengths to further develop the team.*

TC2   I reassign members of a group to different tasks/responsibilities to see where they are good at.

—*Cooperates on projects.*

TC3   On issues that relate to my work, I decide on my own even if I am part of a group. (−)

—*Share plans, information, and information sources.*

TC4   I am quite selective when it comes to sharing my information or knowledge with others. (−)

TC5   When I hear that someone else in my team needs resources that I possess, I immediately offer to share some of these resources with him/her.

—*Encourages a friendly and cooperative atmosphere.*

TC6   I encourage others to visit me for support, advice, or encouragement.

—*Detects and acts on opportunities to cooperate.*

(continues)

Exhibit 4.3   **Continued**

Teamwork and Cooperation (TC) (continued)

TC7   During work meetings I take the initiative to meet the new people that are present.

—Shares successes and responsibilities.

TC8   I share the credit with everyone who contributed to the success, even if I was the main contributor.

Flexibility and Adaptation (FA)

—Is flexible with various demands, changing priorities, and fast changes.

FA1   I am uncomfortable when I have to handle several things at once. (−)

FA2   I adapt quickly to changes in my work situation.

—Is flexible in the way he or she sees things.

FA3   I look at issues from the perspectives of different interest groups.

FA4   I avoid listening to other persons' point of view when I have already formed my own opinion. (−)

—Adjusts his or her approach in response to changing circumstances.

FA5   I adjust my approach to changing circumstances.

FA6   I hang on to successful approaches as long as possible, even when I know the circumstances are changing. (−)

---

negative formulations are indicated in Exhibit 4.3 with the negative (−) sign. This means that the results of these behaviors have to be interpreted in the opposite way. For example, a positive answer on behavior AT2, "My 'intuition' and feelings guide the decisions that I finally make (−)," indicates that this manager relies on his or her feelings and thus *not* on his analytical capabilities. Consequently, this manager does not behave in an analytical manner when using the performance management system.

The assumption is that the self-constructed questionnaire can be applied to measure the management styles a manager displays if he or she is using a performance management system. Again, just as with the Doll and Torkzadeh questionnaire, this assumption must be verified before commencing with testing further assumptions.

ASSUMPTIONS

An actively used performance management system has a distinct influence on managers' performance. However, due to the many interrelated factors that contribute to organizational performance, it is difficult to attribute a direct causal relationship between the use of information and indicators of organizational performance such as profits or sales growth. It is, therefore, best to focus on a particular technology to identify the (perceived) impact of the specific information provided by the technology, rather than the impact of information in general. The focus here is then on the use and impact of a performance management system.

The link between performance management system use, management styles, and organizational performance can be seen in the light of this definition for performance: "The performance domain is defined as the set of behaviors that are relevant to the goals of the organization or organizational unit in which a person works."[3] Another, maybe even better definition is: "Performance consists of goal-relevant actions that are under control of the individual, regardless of whether they are cognitive, motor, psychomotor or interpersonal."[4]

System or contextual factors also have an influence on what people accomplish and on how they behave. There are several factors that, if combined, determine the impact of a performance management system on organizational performance. These include the organizational context in which the performance management system is used, the use made of the performance management system in the evaluation process, the degree of alignment between the performance management system and organizational objectives, and the individual's motivational response to the performance management system. In addition to this, four factors shape managerial behavior in organizations: the corporate culture; the formal structure, systems, plans and policies; leadership; and the competitive and regulatory environment.[5]

It can be expected from managers that they are able to judge whether or not use of the performance management system has a positive influence on their performance. According to the expectancy theory, if a manager is of the opinion that using the performance management system is indeed beneficial, he or she will be willing to use the performance management system. This willingness becomes stronger when the expected benefits of using the performance management system are higher. This, in turn, leads to the actual use of the performance management system, which then leads to the expected improved organizational performance. If management styles and types of performance management system use are inserted in the schematic overview of the book setup (given in Exhibit I.1), a so-called causal flow model is created (Exhibit 4.4).

In the causal flow model, management styles influence both the types of performance management system use managers apply and organizational performance. The types of performance management system use can also influence organizational performance. The organizational envi-

Exhibit 4.4   Causal Flow Model

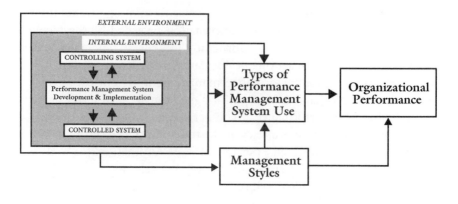

Source: Adapted from Spencer, L. M. Jr., and S. M. Spencer (1993). *Competence at work: Models for superior performance.* New York: John Wiley & Sons.

ronment, specifically the nature of the organization (internal), influences the types of performance management system use managers apply in that organization. The causal flow model gives rise to several assumptions:

Assumption 1:	*Specific management styles are related to specific types of performance management system use.*
Assumption 2:	*A manager's use of a performance management system influences organizational performance favorably.*
Assumption 3:	*Specific management styles influence organizational performance favorably.*

DETAILING OF MANAGEMENT STYLES

To obtain meaningful results, assumption 1 *(Specific management styles are related to specific types of performance management system use)* should be further specified. For this, several management models described in the literature were examined. These management models are in general aiming to map, identify, and subsequently explain the factors that influence the effectiveness of managers' leadership. It is interesting to hypothesize on the basis of these theoretical models which specific management styles give the highest chance on which specific types of performance management system use. This theoretical profile of a performance management system user is assembled by trying to match the descriptions of the management models with the performance management system uses and management styles described in the previous sections, and then deriving the common denominator.

The first management model discussed here is that of Mintzberg, who distinguished eight types of managers.[6] In Exhibit 4.5, these eight types are described and juxtaposed to the performance management system uses and management styles that seem to fit best the descriptions of Mintzberg's manager types. This comparison is made on the basis of the

Exhibit 4.5 **Juxtaposing Mintzberg's Manager Types with Performance Management System Uses (PMS) and Management Styles (MS)**

Manager Type	Description	PMS	MS
Contact person	This manager spends a great deal of time outside of the organization, tries to win orders or obtain exclusive information, and endeavors to strengthen the reputation of the organization.	CO	C
Entrepreneur	This manager is continuously looking for new possibilities and opportunities for the organization, and implements many changes in the organization.	DS	FA
Expert	This manager is an expert and advisor in a particular area.	DS	AT, CT
Insider	This manager is concerned with managing the internal operations of the organization.	WI	TC
New manager	This manager is new in his or her function and, therefore, is mainly concerned with obtaining information and building a relationship network.	CO	C
Political manager	This manager spends a great deal of time outside of the organization in order to reconcile the political forces in the organization.	CO	C
Real-time manager	This manager is also concerned with managing the internal operations of the organization, but mainly focuses on dealing with disturbances and problem solving.	WI	FA, AT
Team manager	This manager is also concerned with managing the internal operations of the organization, but mainly focuses on creating and maintaining an effective team.	WI	TC

factors for performance management system use and management style, which are developed in the next chapter.[7]

Quinn distinguishes several leadership roles and links these with competencies needed by a manager to excel in a particular leadership role.[8] These leadership roles are seen as a function of the orientation of the manager (internal or external) and the prevailing control style of the manager (flexible vs. tight control). The resulting combinations are given labels as can be seen in Exhibit 4.6.

Exhibit 4.7 gives a short description of each leadership role by giving the main characteristics of each role and the main competencies that a manager needs to be able to fulfil this role. A comparison is made of the performance management system uses that would probably best support a particular leadership role, and of the management styles that seem to fit best the descriptions of the required competencies.

An important stream in the literature about leadership models is formed by the contingency or situational leadership theories. These theories state that leadership styles depend on the circumstances of the leader and his or her organization. Since these circumstances will change, different leadership styles and, therefore, different competencies are

Exhibit 4.6 **Leadership Roles in Quinn's Model**

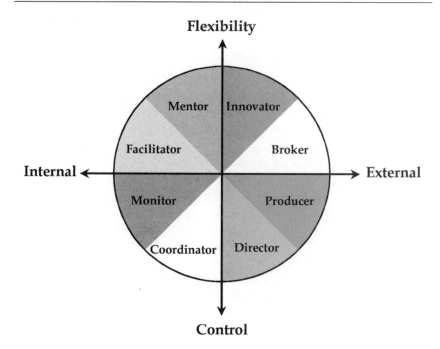

Exhibit 4.7   Juxtaposing Quinn's Leadership Roles with Performance
            Management System Uses (PMS) and Management Styles (MS)

Leadership Role	Characteristics	PMS	Competencies Required	MS
Mentor	■ Has high self-awareness ■ Focuses on developing subordinates ■ Is approachable and caring	WI	■ Understanding of self and others ■ Communicating effectively ■ Developing subordinates	C
Facilitator	■ Supports and develops the team ■ Communicates and follows up on team goals ■ Promotes team spirit and teamwork ■ Deals with conflicts	WI	■ Building teams ■ Using participative decision making ■ Managing conflict	TC, C
Monitor	■ Knows what is going on in the organization ■ Focuses on details, control, and analyses ■ Installs information and control systems	WI	■ Reducing information (overload) ■ Analyzing information through critical thinking ■ Presenting information, writing effectively	AT, CT
Coordinator	■ Manages internal and external projects ■ Develops working procedures and routines ■ Manages contacts between divisions, groups, and departments	WI	■ Managin schedules ■ Organizing	C
Director	■ Defines goals and strategies for the business ■ Plans the business ■ Defines roles and responsibilities	DS	■ Visioning, planning, and goal setting ■ Designing and organizing ■ Delegating effectively	CT, C

(continues)

Exhibit 4.7   **Continued**

Leadership Role	Characteristics	PMS	Competencies Required	MS
Producer	■ Creates guidelines and procedures ■ Focuses on issues, based on short-term and long-term goals ■ Uses time efficiently	WI	■ Orienting on task and result ■ Taking responsibility ■ Managing time and stress	FA
Broker	■ Organizes ■ Maintains and develops external relationships ■ Negotiates and makes deals, both internally and externally	DS	■ Building and maintaining a power base ■ Negotiating agreement and commitment ■ Presenting ideas	C
Innovator	■ Enables changes ■ Manages changes and resistance to changes ■ Creates visions	WI	■ Thinking creatively ■ Creating change ■ Living with change	FA, C

needed. This means that either the manager is able to adapt his or her leadership style or that different managers are required at different times during the life cycle of the organization. Reddin/Hersey and Blanchard have developed models, in which they included the dimensions of task orientation and relation orientation as aspects of situational leadership (Exhibit 4.8).[9]

In Exhibit 4.9, the performance management system uses and management styles factors are juxtaposed with the four leadership styles given in Exhibit 4.8.

Kolb states that successful managers distinguish themselves not so much based on special knowledge or skills, but on their ability to deal flexibly with the continuously changing demands of their job and career.[10] This means these managers possess the skills to explore new possibilities and to learn from past successes and mistakes. Kolb formulated a model that looked at the way managers learn and the resulting learning and managing styles, resulting in four types of manager. In Exhibit 4.10, descriptions of these types are given with an assessment of the performance management system uses and management styles factors that best seem to fit Kolb's manager types.

Exhibit 4.8   The Four Leadership Styles

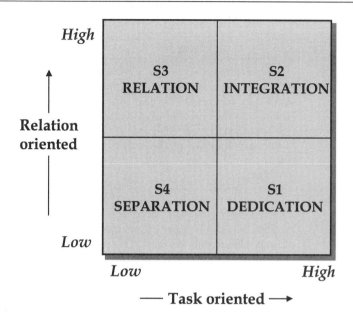

The current trend is that organizations move from a functional to a process orientation with increasing emphasis on cross-functional teams and teamwork and decreasing emphasis on hierarchy. Research shows that a team-based approach to management encourages cross-fertilization of ideas and promotes innovation.[11] When an organization adopts a process orientation, the need to develop and trust individuals within the organization takes on added emphasis. This takes the shape of an increased emphasis on training, cooperation, flexibility, and teamwork. In these types of environments, the performance management system is used to strengthen the exchange of information in a team environment about decisions made, reasons for these decisions, critical activities to be performed, and achieved results. True participative decision making and employee empowerment assist the learning organization, and these processes should be set in place to encourage participation. This will refocus performance measurement to lower levels in the organization, with employees taking responsibility for their decisions and being held accountable for the outcomes. However, it has to be taken into account that cooperation and trust take on a greater importance in both a turbulent environment and in a setting where the decision-making system is group oriented, rather than in a more predictable environment. This is due to the need to share information about environmental changes so

Exhibit 4.9   **Juxtaposing the Leadership Styles of Reddin/Hersey and Blanchard with Performance Management System Uses (PMS) and Management Styles (MS)**

Leadership Style	Description	PMS	MS
S1: Dedication	Priority is given to execution of the work. Which work has to be done and how it has to be done is stipulated by the manager. Control on the quality of work can result in reward or punishment. This style is appropriate for certain types of work in crisis situations and when inexperienced workers are involved.	DS, WI	FA
S2: Integration	Focus lies on teamwork and internal interactions. Which work has to be done is stipulated by the manager. How it has to be done is stipulated by the team. This style is appropriate for managing teams that are highly interdependent.	WI	TC, C
S3: Relation	Priority is given to people. Which work has to be done is discussed between manager and employees. How it has to be done is stipulated by the manager. Ideas and input from employees is valued and rewarded. This style is appropriate for certain types of training and coordination work.	CO	FA, C
S4: Separation	Focus lies on procedures. During internal interactions, logic and rational are leading. This style is appropriate when dealing with professionals who can decide what to work on themselves, or in the case of highly routine work, which is surrounded with strict procedures.	WI	AT, CT

that all the members of the group concerned with that phase of the organization's activities are informed. A trend can be noticed in which the performance measurement process appears to be refocusing from results to the process itself. It appears that when an organization adopts a process orientation, the need to develop and trust individuals within the organization takes on added emphasis. Additionally, increased interaction of personnel in the operating core with each other and with individuals who are not part of the core appear to be leading to an increased emphasis on training, cooperation, flexibility, and teamwork. Taking all this

Exhibit 4.10 Juxtaposing Kolb's Manager Types with Performance Management System Uses (PMS) and Management Styles (MS)

Manager Type	Description	PMS	MS
Converger	These managers are proficient at problem solving, making decisions, and implementing ideas. They are not very emotional and rather work with objects than with people.	DS	AT
Diverger	These managers are proficient at thinking about and visualizing alternatives, and looking at a situation from different angles. They are interested in people and are emotional and imaginative.	CO	CT, C
Assimilator	These managers are proficient at inductive reasoning, creating new theoretical models and abstract concepts. They are less people oriented and value more a precise and logical theoretical basis than a practical solution.	DS	CT
Accommodator	These managers are proficient at the execution of the planning and its related tasks. They look for new experiences, new opportunities and new risks, and solve problems by trial and error. They are flexible adapters to new circumstances.	WI	FA

together gives us a predominant performance management system use of work integration and communication, which is matched with the management style of teamwork and cooperation.

Comparison of the various theoretical relations between performance management system uses and management styles resulted in the following overview of management styles:

- Managers with *analytical* and *conceptual thinking* management styles are proficient at solving problems, making decisions, and implementing ideas across the organization. They focus on rationalizing problems and dealing with disturbances in the organization. They try to reduce information overload and are used to identifying cause-and-effect chains and relationships across the organization and systematically comparing the findings. During internal interactions, logical and rational thinking are key for these managers. Conceptual managers are also proficient at thinking about and visualizing alternatives and looking at a situation from different angles. It seems that the performance management system uses *decision support* and *work integration* can best support these managers.

- Managers with a *flexible* and *adaptive* management style are proficient at adapting to the circumstances and particular working environments and individuals and groups of persons. These managers are concerned with managing the internal operations of the organization, but mainly focus on dealing with disturbances and problem solving. Priority is given to execution of the work and to people who have to do that work. It seems that the performance management system uses *decision support, work integration,* and *communication* can best support these managers.

- Managers with a *cooperative* management style are proficient at working in a team-based environment in which cooperating across the organization is prevalent. These managers are concerned with creating and maintaining an effective team across the organization to be able to manage the internal operations of the organization effectively. It seems that the performance management system uses *work integration* can best support these managers.

- Managers with a *communicative* management style are proficient at interacting effectively with people inside and outside the organization. These managers can spend a great deal of time outside of the organization to try to win orders or obtain exclusive information and to strengthen the reputation of the organization. They are adept at managing internal and external projects. Their focus lies on teamwork and internal interactions, and priority is given to people. It seems that the performance management system uses *work integration* and *communication* can best support these managers.

Assumption 1 *(Specific management styles are related to specific types of performance management system use)* can now be specified further. This is done by combining management styles with particular types of performance management system use, as provided by the assessments made of the theoretical management models. The following assumptions are constructed:

Assumption 1a:	*Analytical thinking management style is related to decision support and work integration types of performance management system use.*
Assumption 1b:	*Conceptual thinking management style is related to decision support and work integration types of performance management system use.*

Assumption 1c: *Flexibility and adaptation management style is related to decision support, work integration, and communication types of performance management system use.*

Assumption 1d: *Teamwork and cooperation management style is related to work integration type of performance management system use.*

Assumption 1e: *Communication management style is related to work integration and communication types of performance management system use.*

ORGANIZATIONAL PERFORMANCE

With regard to assumption 2 *(A manager's use of a performance management system influences organizational performance favorably)*, Kaplan and Norton explicitly predict a favorable effect on the performance in the innovation area.[12] Using a performance management system is predicted to foster a focus on innovation throughout the whole organization. CSFs and KPIs characteristically focus on nonfinancial data. Innovation per definition is nonfinancial in nature because the financial benefit from new ideas, if any, often can be noticed only after a significant time span. The BSC has a perspective called *innovation,* which focuses managers continuously on being innovative.

Paying attention to innovation in this way by using performance indicators and the innovation perspective results in better performance on this aspect. As Kaplan and Norton state: "The learning and growth initiatives are the ultimate drivers of strategic outcomes."[13] However, the literature does not spell out which particular type of performance management system use has the favorable effect on the performance in the innovation area. The fourth assumption is:

Assumption 4:   *A manager's use of a performance management system influences the level of innovation favorably.*

Good performance measures promote cooperation both horizontally and vertically throughout the organization. In this respect, team-based environments are best equipped for effective rollout of the scorecard. This makes the team-based approach to management supportive of cross-fertilization of ideas and promotion of innovation. Local initiatives are encouraged, with performance measured at a local level and an understanding culture that recognizes there will be some failures; there is freedom to make mistakes. Successful teams require the empowerment of team members, an adequate information base, rewards for team performance, and the requisite abilities in team members. Teams that feature performance measurement, with both financial and nonfinancial indicators, and that encourage team members to participate in developing performance targets, perform better than those that do not. However, it must be kept in mind that in a team-based structure measures should be agreed on and monitored by the teams, not by top management. In fact, if superiors start to interfere on the basis of evidence from their own measures (by demanding changes), the whole delicate edifice of the team-based system might well be undermined and could possibly collapse. This leads to the following assumption:

Assumption 5:   *Teamwork and cooperation management style influences organizational performance favorably.*

TYPE OF ORGANIZATION

The nonprofit sector, in general, lags behind in comparison with the for-profit sector in applying CSFs, KPIs, and the BSC and, therefore, has yet to achieve the same benefits as the for-profit sector.[14] Reasons for this are, among others, that applying performance management in the nonprofit sector tends to be more difficult than in the profit sector and that public sector managerial behavior is not yet attuned (enough) to performance management. Fortunately, the public sector is trying hard to catch up to the for-profit sector as the increasing number of articles, reports, and manuals that are specially written for the nonprofit sector indicates.

Manufacturing organizations have a long history, starting with Taylor, of measuring their production processes. The implementation of total quality management (TQM) was another great boost for the measurement movement. Due to these developments, the transition to performance indicators came naturally. Kaplan and Norton reported that the first organizations that converted to the BSC were predominantly manufacturing companies.[15] Research into the relationship between intensity of market competition and business unit performance, and the role that information provided by the performance management system played into this, indicate that the intensity of market competition is a determinant of the use of the information, which in turn is a determinant of business unit performance.[16] An interpretation of the results is that those organizations that use the information can effectively face competition in the market and, thereby, improve performance.

The literature does predict that a performance management system will be used more in for-profit and manufacturing environments than in nonprofit and nonmanufacturing environments. However, which particular types of performance management system use are applied more often is not explicitly predicted. The two assumptions with regard to organizational type are:

> *Assumption 6:*   *A performance management system is used more often in the for-profit sector than in the nonprofit sector.*
>
> *Assumption 7:*   *A performance management system is used more often in manufacturing companies than in non-manufacturing companies.*

AGE AND EXPERIENCE OF MANAGERS

According to the literature, performance management system use has no relationship to the age and experience of the respondents. The assumption is therefore:

> *Assumption 8:*   *The age and experience of a manager do not affect the use of a performance management system.*

Management style and behavior can be linked to the management level on which the person is operating. There is a stream of research that states that the required management styles for using a PMS differ per management level, as follows[17]:

- *Conceptual skills.* Top managers who formulate strategy and policy need to possess conceptual skills in order to be able to form a picture about the opportunities of the organization in relation to its environment. These top managers also have to be able to judge the merit of these opportunities and to make predictions on the basis of these.
- *Human relations skills.* Top managers need to create charisma, which then creates trust in the leader. For this, a certain distance has to be created between leader and followers. Middle managers, however, need powers of persuasion and social skills and need to be able to create warmth. They depend on personal sympathy and the

respect of their employees. Lower-level managers have to deal straightforwardly and honestly with their subordinates.

■ *Technical skills.* Middle managers need, more than top managers, knowledge of and experience with internal systems in order to implement the strategy effectively. Lower-level managers need especially technical know-how.

The literature states that every manager, regardless of his or her level in the organization, needs to possess all the described skills to a certain degree. However, possessing certain skills is more important on specific levels to become successful. This leads to the following assumption:

Assumption 9:   *The need for conceptual skills is linked to management level.*

In the next chapter, the assumptions are tested on the basis of a survey into the management styles of managers and their types of performance management system use.

ENDNOTES

1. Doll, W. J., and G. Torkzadeh (1998). "Developing a multidimensional measure of system-use in an organizational context." *Information and Management* 33:171–185.
2. Hirschhorn, E., and K. Farduhar (1985). "Productivity, technology and the decline of the autonomous professional." *Office Technology and People* 2:245–265.
3. Murphy, K. R. (1990). "Job performance and productivity." In: Murphy, K. R., and F. E. Saal, eds., *Psychology in organizations*. Hillsdale, NJ: Erlbaum.
4. Campbell, J. P., R. A. McCloy, S. H. Oppler, and C. E. Sager (1993). "A theory of performance." In: W. C. Borman and Associates. *Personnel selection in organizations*. San Franciso: Jossey-Bass.
5. Kotter, J. P., and J. L. Heskett (1992). *Corporate culture and performance*. New York: The Free Press.
6. Mintzberg, H. (1973). *The nature of managerial work*. Upper Saddle River, NJ: Prentice Hall; Mintzberg, H. (1983). *Power in and around organizations*. Upper Saddle River, NJ: Prentice Hall; Mintzberg, H. (1983). *Structures in fives*. Upper Saddle River, NJ: Prentice Hall International.
7. In Chapter 5, the performance management system uses and management styles are converted into factors using statistical analysis. These factors are, for convenience sake, already used here. They are performance management

system use factors (decision support, DS; work integration, WI; and communication, CO) and management style factors (analytical thinking, AT; conceptual thinking, CT; teamwork and cooperation, TC; flexibility and adaptation, FA; and communication, C).

8. Quinn, R. E., S. R. Faerman, M. P. Thompson, and M. R. McGrath (1990). *Becoming a master manager: A competency framework.* New York: John Wiley & Sons.

9. Reddin, W. J. (1977). *Effective MBO.* Samsom, Alphen aan den Rijn, Hersey, P., and K. H. Blanchard (1982). *Management of organizational behavior.* Upper Saddle River, NJ: Prentice Hall.

10. Kolb, D. A., J. M. Rubin, and J. M. McIntyre (1984). *Organizational psychology: Readings on human behavior in organizations.* Upper Saddle River, NJ: Prentice Hall.

11. Johnston, R., and L. Fitzgerald (2000). "Performance measurement: Flying in the face of fashion." In: A. Neely, ed., *Performance measurement—past, present and future.* Cranfield: Centre for Business Performance, Cranfield University, 275–282.

12. Kaplan, R. S., and D. P. Norton (1996). *The balanced scorecard: Translating strategy into action.* Boston: Harvard Business School Press.

13. Kaplan, R. S., and D. P. Norton (2000). *The strategy-focused organization: How balanced scorecard companies thrive in the new business environment.* Boston: Harvard Business School Press.

14. Atkinson, A. A., and J. Q. McCrindell (1997). "Strategic performance measurement in government." *CMA Magazine.* April; Smith, P. (1995). "On the unintended consequences of publishing performance data in the public sector." *International Journal of Public Administration* 18, 2/3:277–310.

15. Kaplan and Norton. *The balanced scorecard: Translating strategy into action.*

16. Mia, L., and B. Clarke (1999). "Market competition, management accounting systems and business unit performance." *Management Accounting Research* 10:137–158.

17. Katz, D., and R. L. Kahn (1978). *The social psychology of organizations.* New York: John Wiley & Sons.

5

PERFORMANCE MANAGEMENT SYSTEM AND MANAGERIAL BEHAVIOR SURVEY

In Chapter 4, specific management styles that managers theoretically should display to make frequent, day-to-day use of a performance management system for specific purposes, were identified during a literature study. In addition, assumptions were formulated about the relations between the identified performance management system use factors and management styles. In this chapter, a description is given of how a survey is used to test these assumptions at 11 organizations.

DESCRIPTION OF THE SURVEY

For the survey, the questionnaire on measures of performance management system use, adapted from Doll and Torkzadeh (Exhibit 4.2) was combined with the questionnaire on management styles (Exhibit 4.3) and with general questions about age, sex, and management experience. In order to limit the number of socially desirable answers, the questions were alternatively formulated in a positive and a negative way. This resulted in a self-constructed questionnaire, which is given in Appendix B.

Potentially suitable organizations were selected on the basis of two criteria. The first criterion was that the participating organization should have a balanced performance management system at its disposal for at least two to three years. This means the performance management system contains financial as well as nonfinancial information, in the shape of critical success factors (CSFs), key performance indicators (KPIs), and/or the balanced scorecard (BSC). The reason for using the time limit is the potentially disruptive changes a performance management system implementation can bring (resistance, cultural barriers, change management issues). These issues could distort the perception of users about their performance management systems. The assumption was that after a period of approximately two years, the situation surrounding the performance management system should have settled down enough for users to give answers in a fairly objective way. The second criterion was a pragmatic one: Either I or one of my colleagues should have contacts at the candidate organization.

The organizations that participated in the survey are described in Exhibit 5.1. Characteristics given are: the organizational level of the participating units (headquarters or business unit), the industry type (for-profit or nonprofit), whether it is a manufacturing type or a service type of organization, and whether it concerns a multinational or a national organization. The "Size" column indicates whether the participating unit was large or small in headcount. In the "Quest." column, the number of questionnaires distributed in the organization is given; in the "Return" column, the number and percentage of returned questionnaires is given.

At three companies, additional open interviews with 10 managers were conducted. The purpose of these interviews was to gather additional information about how these managers used their organization's performance management system and to check consistency between the answers of the questionnaire and what managers told us. In addition, the behaviors and management styles of effective performance management system users were discussed in more detail with the interviewees.

ANALYSIS OF THE SURVEY

In this section, a description is given of how the various assumptions regarding the possibility of using the Doll and Torkzadeh questionnaire (to measure types of performance management system use) and the self-constructed questionnaire (to measure management styles needed for specific type of performance management system use) were tested. In Chapter 4, it was assumed that the Doll and Torkzadeh questionnaire could be applied to measure the various types of performance management system use of managers. It was assumed that the self-constructed questionnaire could be applied to measure the management styles that managers display when they are using a performance management system. These two assumptions have been verified before commencing the testing of the assumptions developed. In this section, the results of the verification are discussed.

Analysis of Performance Management System Use

By means of factor analysis, the underlying factors in a set of components can be identified. Doll and Torkzadeh used a principal component analysis (PCA) to put together their "measures of system use" questionnaire (see Exhibit 4.2). This type of analysis was repeated to establish whether or not the same components of performance management system use as found by Doll and Torkzadeh (problem solving, decision rationalization, horizontal integration, vertical integration, and customer service) could also be identified in this research. In this way, the assumption that the Doll and Torkzadeh questionnaire could be applied to measure the various types of performance management system use of managers would be verified.

This analysis is interesting because the Doll and Torkzadeh questionnaire was originally meant to measure systems use of a management information system (MIS), not performance management system use. This means that there is a possibility that the adapted Doll and Torkzadeh questionnaire as used in this study displays different factors if it is employed to measure uses of a performance management system. Since Doll and Torkzadeh identified five factors, it was assumed that the PCA would also result in five factors. The results of this PCA are summarized in Exhibit 5.2.

The first factor, containing all 22 components (with loadings between .860 and .672), is basically a combination of *all* the adapted Doll and Torkzadeh components together. The Doll and Torkzadeh questionnaire is based on the assumption that one can clearly identify the different types of MIS use of managers. In contrast, the PCA for the adapted Doll and Torkzadeh questionnaire shows that the respondents of the survey basically use the performance management system for all its purposes. Since all the components, without exception, load higher than .670 on the first factor, no real difference can be made between the various types of performance management system use as postulated in the adapted Doll and Torkzadeh questionnaire. The PCA outcome fits with the main activity of a manager, namely managing. Managing basically consists of a collection of various activities, which deal with internal processes, external relations, human aspects, and (especially) communication. All these activities are supported by a well-designed performance management system (see the literature overview in Chapter 1).

For further analysis, it is useful to perform additional factor analyses. The grouping of components in factors is finalized in such a way that an interpretable structure is created. The results are summarized in Exhibit 5.3.

The analysis results in a three-factor structure with some components loading on several factors. The first factor, named *decision support* (DS),

Exhibit 5.1 Description of the Participating Organizations

Organization	Description	Level	Quest.	Return	Industry	Type	Sort	Size
Philips Lighting	Lighting product manufacturer	Business unit	60	51 (85%)	Profit	Manufacturing	Multinational	Large
Corus	Steel and aluminium manufacturer	Business unit	20	12 (60%)	Profit	Manufacturing	Multinational	Large
SKF Engineering and Research	Research center of ball-bearing manufacturer	Business unit	5	2 (40%)	Profit	Nonmanufacturing	Multinational	Small
Bass Brewers	Distiller	Head-quarters	4	1 (25%)	Profit	Manufacturing	National (U.K.)	Small
Cadbury Schweppes	Distiller	Head-quarters	3	1 (33%)	Profit	Manufacturing	National (U.K.)	Small
Andersen Business Consulting	Consultancy firm	Business unit	10	9 (90%)	Profit	Nonmanufacturing	Multinational	Small
CSM Levensmiddelen	Food producer	Business unit	4	2 (50%)	Profit	Manufacturing	Multinational	Large
DHL	Transport company	Business unit	2	1 (50%)	Profit	Nonmanufacturing	Multinational	Small

Wessanen	Food producer	Business unit	12	8 (67%)	Profit	Manufacturing	Multinational	Large
Xerox	Document company	Business unit	3	1 (33%)	Profit	Manufacturing	Multinational	Large
WBV Het Oosten	Social housing association	Head-quarters	28	23 (82%)	Nonprofit	Nonmanufacturing	National (Netherlands)	Small
Centrale Financiën Instellingen	Governmental agency	Head-quarters	13	10 (77%)	Nonprofit	Nonmanufacturing	National (Netherlands)	Small
Total			164	121 (74%)				

Exhibit 5.2 **Principal Component Analysis of Performance Management System Use Components (Five Components)**

No.	Performance Management System Components	1	2	3	4	5
				Factors		
V4	I use the performance management system to communicate with people who report to me.	.860				
R7	I use the performance management system to make the decision process more rational.	.856				
C3	I use the performance management system to improve the quality of customer service.	.837				
R6	I use the performance management system to improve the effectiveness and efficiency of the decision process.	.823				
H1	I use the performance management system to communicate with other people in my work group.	.813				
H2	My work group and I use the performance management system to coordinate our activities.	.813	−.325			
C4	I use the performance management system to serve customers more creatively.	.808				
R3	I use the performance management system to help me make explicit the reasons for my decisions.	.801				
R1	I use the performance management system to help me explain my decisions.	.799				
V5	I use the performance management system to communicate with people to whom I report.	.795		−.417		

Exhibit 5.2 **Continued**

		Factors				
No.	*Performance Management System Components*	*1*	*2*	*3*	*4*	*5*
H3	I use the performance management system to coordinate activities with others in my work group.	**.793**				−.330
V8	I use the performance management system to get feedback on job performance.	**.784**				
C2	I use the performance management system to serve internal and/or external customers.	**.783**				−.331
P4	I use the performance management system to check my thinking against the data.	**.779**				
C1	I use the performance management system to deal more strategically with internal and/or external customers.	**.767**	−.384			
V2	I use the performance management system to monitor my own performance.	**.763**				
R2	I use the performance management system to help me justify my decisions.	**.746**				
V3	I use the performance management system to plan my work.	**.741**			−.407	
P5	I use the performance management system to make sense out of the data.	**.714**			.354	
C5	I use the performance management system to exchange information with internal and/or external customers.	**.698**	−.459			
P1	I use the performance management system to decide how best to approach a problem.	**.681**				.303
P6	I use the performance management system to analyze why problems occur.	**.672**			.530	

Exhibit 5.3   **Principal Component Analysis of Performance Management System Use Components (Three Components)**

No.	Performance Management System Components	DS	WI	CO
			Factor	
R2	I use the performance management system to help me justify my decisions.	.481		−.386
R3	I use the performance management system to help me make explicit the reasons for my decisions.	.459		−.490
R6	I use the performance management system to improve the effectiveness and efficiency of the decision process.	.649		
R7	I use the performance management system to make the decision process more rational.	.541		
P1	I use the performance management system to decide how best to approach a problem.	.777		
P4	I use the performance management system to check my thinking against the data.	.897		
P5	I use the performance management system to make sense out of the data.	.656		
P6	I use the performance management system to analyze why problems occur.	.662		
V3	I use the performance management system to plan my work.	.674		
C4	I use the performance management system to serve customers more creatively.	.705	−.306	
H1	I use the performance management system to communicate with other people in my work group.		.450	.554
H2	My work group and I use the performance management system to coordinate our activities.		.599	.345
H3	I use the performance management system to coordinate activities with others in my work group.		.533	
C1	I use the performance management system to deal more strategically with internal and/or external customers.	−.344	.658	
C2	I use the performance management system to serve internal and/or external customers.	−.496	.436	
C3	I use the performance management system to improve the quality of customer service.	−.447	.320	
C5	I use the performance management system to exchange information with internal and/or external customers.		.726	

Exhibit 5.3   **Continued**

			Factor	
No.	Performance Management System Components	DS	WI	CO
V2	I use the performance management system to monitor my own performance.			.778
V4	I use the performance management system to communicate with people who report to me.			.678
V5	I use the performance management system to communicate with people to whom I report.			.910
V8	I use the performance management system to get feedback on job performance.			.711
R1	I use the performance management system to help me explain my decisions.			.770

matches almost completely the Doll and Torkzadeh MIS use factors "problem solving" and "decision rationalization" taken together, matching their system use term *decision support* (see Exhibit 4.1). Component R3 ("I use the performance management system to help me make explicit the reasons for my decisions"), which loads equally well on factors DS and communication (CO), has been added to factor DS because this component seems to be more relevant for rationalizing decisions. Components C2 and C3, both loading on factor DS as well as on factor WI *(work integration)*, were removed from factor DS and added to factor WI, creating an even better overlap with the Doll and Torkzadeh questionnaire. There are two components in factor DS that do not match the original Doll and Torkzadeh grouping. First, component V3 ("I use the performance management system to plan my work") could well belong to factor DS because planning one's work can be seen as making decisions about the order and priority of activities. Second, component C4 ("I use the performance management system to serve customers more creatively") can be seen as a specific example of a problem that has to be solved: how to better serve the customer. By viewing the component in this way, it clearly belongs to factor DS.

The second factor, *work integration* (WI), matches almost completely the Doll and Torkzadeh MIS use factors "horizontal integration" and "customer service" taken together with only component C4 missing. Factor WI can be viewed as a process improvement factor with the process of servicing the customer being just another one of those processes that have to be performed well in an integrated way by manager and team. For this reason, components C2 ("I use the performance management system to serve internal and/or external customers") and C3 ("I use the performance management system to improve the quality of customer service") can be added to factor WI because they both deal with the customer servicing process.

Finally, the third factor, *communication* (CO), matches the Doll and Torkzadeh MIS use factor "vertical integration" with the addition of component R1 ("I use the performance management system to help me explain my decisions"). This component can clearly be seen as part of a communication process, complementing components V4 and V5. For this reason, the Doll and Torkzadeh MIS use factor "vertical integration" was renamed in this investigation to "communication."

In summary, it can be concluded that using the Doll and Torkzadeh questionnaire is justified as a basis for measuring the use of a performance management system. Consequently, the assumption that the Doll and Torkzadeh questionnaire can be applied to measure the various types of performance management system use of managers has been proven correct.

Analysis of Management Styles

A PCA was used to verify the assumption that the self-constructed questionnaire could be applied to measure the management styles associated with certain types of performance management system use. With this method, common factors were looked for in the measured components. This analysis is needed because the management styles have been grouped arbitrarily in the self-constructed questionnaire. It, therefore, has to be checked whether another, more logical grouping is possible. It was assumed that the PCA would result in five factors. In order to increase the reliability of the outcomes, I decided after several trial runs to remove components that either loaded lower than .3 on a factor, loaded almost equally on more than one factor, or loaded on a factor that could not be logically explained. In this way, components AT5, AT6, AT7, AT8, C4, C5, FA3, FA4, FA6, TC4, TC5, and CT6 were removed. The results of the analysis are summarized in Exhibit 5.4.

The first factor, *conceptual thinking* (CT), matches the original grouping "conceptual thinking." Only component CT1 ("I understand new things by seeing how they fit with what I already know") does not load on this factor. There is one additional component that loads significantly on this factor: component AT3 ("When trying to understand a problem, I work it out to identify its different aspects"). This indicates the competency to break down a problem in its underlying parts is more

Exhibit 5.4   **Principal Component Analysis of Management Style Components (Five Components)**

		Factor				
No.	*Management Style Components*	*CT*	*FA*	*TC*	*C*	*AT*
AT3	When trying to understand a problem, I work it out to identify its different aspects.	.790				
CT2	When performing a task that is new to me, I first investigate how it is related to other tasks that I performed in the past.	.517				
CT3	I combine relevant information and concepts from several very different sources to get a clear picture of the situation.	.742				−.306
CT4	When I need to assess a situation, I look at the information available. (−)	.493		.313		
CT5	When I want to solve a complex problem, I try to redefine it into concepts that are recognizable to me.	.331				
C2	When someone is speaking to me (or to an audience that I am part of), I am able to stop thinking instantly about anything else and concentrate on what is being said.		.690			
FA1	I am uncomfortable when I have to handle several things at once. (−)		−.477			
FA2	I adapt quickly to changes in my work situation.		.735			
FA5	I adjust my approach to changing circumstances.		.603		−.380	
TC7	During work meetings, I take the initiative to meet the new people who are present.		.442		−.336	
TC1	I encourage others in the group to work together.			.778		
TC6	I encourage others to visit me for support, advice, or encouragement.			.670		
TC8	I share the credit with everyone, who contributed to a success, even if I was the main contributor.			.717		

(continues)

Exhibit 5.4 **Continued**

No.	Management Style Components	CT	FA	TC	C	AT
				Factor		
C1	I repeat something that someone says to me in my own words to ensure that I have understood the message correctly.				.583	
C3	I have a variety of writing styles from which I choose the most appropriate for the reader whom I am addressing my correspondence to.				.387	
C6	I pay particular attention to others' feelings when expressing myself.				.608	
CT1	I understand new things by seeing how they fit with what I already know.				.512	
TC2	I reassign members of a group to different tasks/responsibilities to see where they are good at.				.320	
TC3	On issues that relate to my work, I decide on my own even if I am part of a group. (−)				−.624	
AT1	I make rational decisions even if my feelings tell me to make alternative ones.					.836
AT2	My intuition and feelings guide the decisions that I finally make. (−)					−.826

conceptual than analytical in nature. The initial meaning of the switched component CT4 ("When I need to assess a situation, I look at the information available (−)") was that a manager should not only look at the information on hand but should also collect and analyze other relevant information. This component has a positive load, indicating that the respondents could have interpreted the question as follows: a manager first looks at all the information available before starting to think conceptually about a problem.

The second factor, *flexibility and adaptation* (FA), matches partially to the original grouping "flexibility and adaptation." The extra components, which load strongly on this factor, are indications of a flexible and adaptive style. Component C2 ("When someone is speaking to me, I am able to stop thinking instantly about anything else and concentrate on what is being said") and TC7 ("During work meetings I take the initiative to meet the new people who are present") indicate the manner in which a manager is flexible, either by directly adapting oneself to a situation or by being open to new team members.

The third factor, *teamwork and cooperation* (TC), matches the original grouping "teamwork and cooperation." Components TC2, TC3, and TC7 load on other factors than factor TC and are not categorized under factor TC.

The fourth factor, *communication* (C), matches the original grouping "communication." The extra components that load strongly on this factor are indications of a communicative style. Reassigning members of one group to different tasks (component TC2) can be done only in dialogue with the team members. Component TC3 ("On issues that relate to my work, I decide on my own even if I am part of a group. (–)") loads negatively, meaning that the manager takes decisions after conferring with the other team members. Component CT1 ("I understand new things by seeing how they fit with what I already know") seems to be the odd one out. However, it may be that the manager communicates with the other team members about the new things and how they fit in what the team knows, to get a better understanding.

The fifth factor, *analytical thinking* (AT), matches to the original grouping "analytical thinking." Component AT2 ("My 'intuition' and feelings guide the decisions that I finally make. (–)"), which has been switched (i.e., formulated in a negative way), has a negative load, meaning it supports this factor. Component AT3 ("When trying to understand a problem, I work it out to identify its different aspects") loads stronger on another factor and is, therefore, not categorized under factor AT but under factor CT.

In summary, using the self-constructed questionnaire as a basis for measuring the management styles needed for performance management system use is justified, after making some changes. These changes consist mainly of regrouping some components, while a number of components were excluded from further analysis (by not grouping them under a factor). Consequently, the assumption that the self-constructed questionnaire can be applied to measure the management styles that a manager needs to possess in order to be able to use the performance management system has been proven to be correct.

RESULTS OF THE SURVEY

Now that it has been established that the self-constructed questionnaire can be used for measuring the management styles needed for performance management system use, the various assumptions can be tested. This is done by looking at whether correlations exist between the measures of performance management system use, the management styles, and organizational performance.

Correlation Between Performance Management System Use and Management Style Factors

After identifying the performance management system use factors and management style factors, the correlation between the two types of factors was calculated in order to test various assumptions. In Exhibit 5.5, for each performance management system use factor (derived from Exhibit 5.3), the levels of correlation with the various management style factors (derived from Exhibit 5.4) are given. The higher the value of the correlation, the higher the interdependence between the two factors is. For each correlation, the level of significance is given. The significance indicates whether the correlation between the scale and the component occurred by chance or whether it is structural. The research aims at finding correlations with a significance of less than 0.1. These are correlations of which it can be said with a certainty of 90 to 95% that the correlation between the scale and the component is not accidental. In Exhibit 5.5, the significant correlations have been printed in bold on a shaded background.

The correlation matrix shows there are two significant but weak correlations. This means that assumption 1 *(Specific management styles are*

Exhibit 5.5 **Correlation Matrix of the Performance Management System Use Factors and the Management Style Factors**

Management Style Factors		Performance Management System Use Factors		
		Support	Decision Integration	Work Communication
Conceptual thinking	Correlation	.071	.034	.029
	Significance	.232	.363	.384
Flexibility and adaptation	Correlation	−.035	.100	−.004
	Significance	.357	.153	.483
Teamwork and cooperation	Correlation	−.098	−.101	−.116
	Significance	.158	.150	.116
Communication	Correlation	**.129**	.088	.083
	Significance	**.092**	.185	.197
Analytical thinking	Correlation	.104	.117	**.177**
	Significance	.143	.115	**.034**

related to specific types of performance management system use) cannot be rejected for two management styles. The first correlation is between the management style *communication* and performance management system use for *decision support,* indicating that there exists a relationship between managers with highly developed communication skills and their use of the performance management system for decision-making purposes. It was expected that this management style would have a relationship with the performance management system use communication, but not with decision support. This means that assumption 1e *(Communication management style is related to work integration and communication types of performance management system use)* has to be rejected. It could be that managers need to communicate a lot with the stakeholders, who have an interest in the outcome of the decision-making process, and that the managers use the performance management system to support them in providing the information needed as input for the decision making.

The second significant correlation is the one between the management style *analytical thinking* and the *communication* type of performance management system use. This indicates a relationship exists between managers who are proficient at analytical thinking and their use of the performance management system for sharing information with and communicating their performance to the other team members or their superiors. A possible explanation for this is that people who are analytically inclined need the information from a performance management system to explain their actions to others. This correlation means that assumption 1a *(Analytical thinking management style is related to decision support and work integration types of performance management system use)* has to be rejected because the correlation is with communication, not with decision support or with work integration.

The other assumptions, 1b *(Conceptual thinking management style is related to decision support and work integration types of performance management system use)*, 1c *(Flexibility and adaptation management style is related to decision support, work integration, and communication types of performance management system use)*, and 1d *(Teamwork and cooperation management style is related to work integration type of performance management system use)* are also rejected due to a lack of correlation.

Correlation with the Performance of the Organization

Many organizations implement a performance management system because they expect a better performance as a result of good use. As was discussed in the literature overview in Chapter 1, there is a growing body of anecdotal evidence that supports this expectation. This section not only discusses the relationship between the types of performance management system use and organizational performance, but also the relationship between management styles of managers and organizational performance.

To test assumptions 2 *(A manager's use of a performance management system influences organizational performance favorably)*, 3 *(Specific management styles influence organizational performance favorably)*, and 5 *(Teamwork and cooperation management style is related to a favorable organizational performance)*, the respondents of the survey were asked the following question: "In relation to other comparable organizations or organizational units, how did your unit—in your opinion—rate on each of the following factors during the past year?" The respondents had to answer this question for eight performance components. These components were put together from several literature sources and were put through a principal component analysis to establish the main performance factors (Exhibit 5.6).

The analysis results in a two-factor structure with all components loading on both factors. The first performance factor, *productivity*, consists of components that all load high on this factor and that all have to do with reaching the quantitative goals an organization sets for itself. These are financial (V9_8 and V9_9) and operational (V9_5 and V9_6). Component V9_1, although loading higher on the other factor, has been grouped under PR because, being quantitative, this makes more logical sense.

Exhibit 5.6 **Principal Component Analysis of Performance Components (Two Components)**

		Performance Factors	
No.	*Performance Components*	*Productivity*	*Quality*
V9_1	The quantity or amount of work produced	.333	.467
V9_5	Attainment of unit productions or service goals	.785	−.032
V9_6	Efficiency of unit operations	.629	.238
V9_8	Development of revenues (if applicable)	.814	−.135
V9_9	Development of profits (if applicable)	.842	−.040
V9_2	The quality or accuracy of work produced	.398	.530
V9_3	The number of innovations or new ideas introduced	−.356	.843
V9_4	Reputation for work excellence	.282	.638

The second performance factor, *quality*, consists of components that all load high on this factor and that all have to do with reaching the qualitative goals that an organization sets for itself. This is the quality produced (V9_2 and V9_3) and the quality reputation achieved (V9_4).

After identifying the performance factors, the correlation between these factors and the performance management system use factors, respectively, the management styles factors were calculated. Exhibit 5.7 gives the significant correlations.

The correlation matrix shows that the performance management system use factors are correlated with both performance factors. This indicates that relations exist between all the types of performance management system use and organizational performance. For example, the manager finds it beneficial to use the performance management system to integrate the work processes efficiently, in order to attain the productivity and quality goals. This means that assumption 2 *(A manager's use of a performance management system influences organizational performance favorably)* cannot be rejected.

All management style factors are correlated with one or both performance factors. This indicates that relationships exist between the management styles managers possess and the organizational performance they achieve. The management styles of *conceptual thinking* and *communication* are both needed to attain good performance. The management style factors *flexibility and adaptation* and *teamwork and cooperation* are correlated to one performance factor, indicating that being flexible and adaptive is especially needed in order to achieve modernization of tasks, which is needed to achieve higher quality, and that to obtain a higher productivity, a management style focused on intensive teamwork and close cooperation between work units is especially needed.

The results mean that assumption 3 *(Specific management styles influence organizational performance favorably)* cannot be rejected for four factors. Only *analytical thinking* does not seem to have a relationship with performance. Assumption 5 *(Teamwork and cooperation management style influences organizational performance favorably)* cannot be rejected for the performance factor *productivity*.

To test assumption 4 *(A manager's use of a performance management system influences the level of innovation favorably)*, we correlate component V9_3 ("The number of innovations or new ideas introduced") with the performance management system use and management style factors (Exhibit 5.8).

Clear correlations exist between performance management system use factors, management style factors, and innovation. This indicates a relationship between the use of a performance management system and a

Exhibit 5.7 **Correlation Matrix of the Performance Factors with the Performance Management System Use Factors and Management Style Factors**

		Performance Management System Use Factors			Management Style Factors				
Performance Factors		Decision Support	Work Integration	Communication	Conceptual Thinking	Flexibility & Adaptation	Teamwork & Cooperation	Communication	Analytical Thinking
Productivity	Correlation	.151	.244	.223	.245	.081	.216	.189	-.038
	Significance	.099	.019	.028	.015	.239	.028	.048	.371
Quality	Correlation	.169	.185	.099	.238	.196	.097	.238	.007
	Significance	.041	.028	.155	.006	.019	.156	.006	.472

Exhibit 5.8 **Correlation Matrix of Component V9_3 with the Performance Management System Use Factors and Management Style Factors**

Performance Component		Performance Management System Use Factors			Management Style Factors				
		Decision Support	Work Integration	Communication	Conceptual Thinking	Flexibility & Adaptation	Teamwork & Cooperation	Communication	Analytical Thinking
Number of innovations/ New ideas	Correlation	.229	.250	.118	.193	.207	.080	.202	.033
	Significance	.009	.005	.114	.021	.014	.203	.017	.364

focus on innovation throughout the whole organization. CSFs and KPIs characteristically focus on nonfinancial data. Innovation per definition is nonfinancial in nature because the financial benefit from new ideas, if any, often can be noticed only after a significant time span. The BSC has a separate perspective, called *innovation*, which focuses managers continuously on being innovative. Paying attention to innovation in this way, by using performance indicators and the innovation perspective, results in better performance on this aspect. As Kaplan and Norton state: "The learning and growth initiatives are the ultimate drivers of strategic outcomes."[1]

Consequently, assumption 4 *(A manager's use of a performance management system influences the level of innovation favorably)* cannot be rejected. This is an encouraging result, especially because a large-scale survey of performance management practices found that in particular the innovative perspective of the BSC could be significantly improved (Exhibit 5.9).

It is a fact that managers are still predominantly concerned with financial measures of performance, return on capital employed (ROCE), profit, revenue, share price, and costs. A survey of top European companies found that no matter what respondents said they were trying to achieve, when asked how they were measuring success, the focus was overwhelmingly on cost.[2] A similar observation comes from a recent study that found that most organizations' scorecards are far from balanced. Almost three quarters of the performance measures are financial in nature. The drawback of this is, as the study notes, that "with a BSC that focuses largely on historical results, companies are certainly missing current or potential problems and opportunities that could be brought to light, by also including more internal and external operating measures."[3]

Exhibit 5.9 **Rating of the Quality of the Performance Management System, in the Four Perspectives of the BSC**

BSC Perspective	Poor/Less Than Adequate	Adequate/Good	Very Good/Excellent
Financial	14.0%	50.4%	35.5%
Customer	37.2%	47.9%	14.9%
Internal process	42.9%	48.7%	8.4%
Innovation	53.8%	39.5%	6.7%

Source: Frigo, M. (2000). "Current trends in performance measurement systems." In: Neely, A., ed., *Performance measurement—past, present and future*. Cranfield: Centre for Business Performance, Cranfield University.

Correlation with Organization Type

In this section, the performance management system use factors are related to the different types of organizations. For this analysis, the t-test was used. This test examines the components that have more significance for one group compared to the other group, which shows in a higher value in the "Mean" column. In Exhibit 5.10, the results are given for the relationship between types of performance management system use and the sector type in which the organization operates.

The t-test shows that, in general, for-profit managers use a performance management system more for decision support and work integration purposes than nonprofit managers. The difference between the two sectors is not that significant for the communication use. The result means assumption 6 *(A performance management system is used more often in the for-profit sector than in the nonprofit sector)* cannot be rejected for the decision support and work integration types of performance management system use. This result ties in with the observation that the BSC framework has been gaining support at many companies. Recently, Bain & Company estimated that 55% of the U.S. companies it surveyed and 45% of the European companies use the BSC. According to the IMA performance management system survey, approximately 40% of the respondents are currently using a BSC or plan to within the next year. In the survey, 12% of the companies have been using the BSC for more than two years.[4] Fortunately, the public sector is trying hard to catch up to the profit sector as indicated by an increasing number of articles, reports, and manuals, specifically written for the nonprofit sector.

In Exhibit 5.11, the results are given for the relationship between types of performance management system use and organization type.

Exhibit 5.10 **T-test for Performance Management System Use Factors and Sector Types**

Performance Management System Use Factors	Sector Type	N	Mean	Significance
Decision support	Profit	79	**3.16**	.072
	Nonprofit	31	2.90	
Work integration	Profit	78	**3.26**	.055
	Nonprofit	31	2.94	
Communication	Profit	79	3.45	.141
	Nonprofit	31	3.23	

Exhibit 5.11   T-test for Performance Management System Use Factors and Organizational Types

Performance Management System Use Factors	Organization Type	N	Mean	Significance
Decision support	Manufacturing	69	3.28	.001
	Nonmanufacturing	41	2.76	
Work integration	Manufacturing	68	3.40	.001
	Nonmanufacturing	41	2.79	
Communication	Manufacturing	69	3.58	.004
	Nonmanufacturing	41	3.05	

In general, this t-test shows that production managers use a performance management system more for decision support, work integration, and communication purposes than nonproduction (service, transport) managers. The result means that assumption 7 *(A performance management system is used more often in manufacturing companies than in nonmanufacturing companies)* cannot be rejected for all three types of performance management system use.

Correlation with Age and Experience of Managers

The next relationship to be tested is the one between performance management system use and the age and experience of managers. The results are presented in Exhibit 5.12.

Exhibit 5.12   Correlation Matrix of the Performance Management System Use Factors and Manager Characteristics

Manager Characteristics		PMS Factors		
		Decision Support	Work Integration	Communication
V1_1 Age	Correlation	.083	.127	.090
	Significance	.197	.096	.177
V1_3 Years of experience in current profession	Correlation	.050	.078	−.042
	Significance	.301	.211	.333
V1_4 Years of experience in current function	Correlation	−.008	.049	−.027
	Significance	.467	.306	.391

The correlation matrix in Exhibit 5.12 shows only one significant, but not very strong correlation for item V1_1 ("Age") with the factor *work integration*. There are no other significant correlations, indicating basically that there are no specific age groups or experience groups that use the performance management system for a particular reason. Therefore, assumption 8 *(The age and experience of a manager do not affect the use of a performance management system)* cannot be rejected.

To test assumption 9 *(The need for conceptual skills is linked to management level)*, the respondents were asked how many employees and organizational units they had under their direct and indirect responsibility. The answers were correlated with the management styles factors. The results are given in Exhibit 5.13.

The results show that a relationship exists between size of responsibility area and several management styles. The observation that top managers in particular need to possess conceptual skills but need less communication skills is supported by the results.[5] It also seems that the more organizational units a manager has under his or her indirect responsibility, the less his or her management styles matter—probably due to the distance between the manager and these units. This result means that assumption 6 *(The need for conceptual skills is linked to management level)* cannot be rejected.

INTERVIEW RESULTS

In addition to sending out questionnaires, 10 managers from three different organizations were interviewed. The position of these managers varied among chief executive officer (CEO), chief financial officer (CFO), plant manager, and department head. They all were experienced and had worked quite some time at their organizations, although not necessarily in their latest function. In the interviews, additional information about the organization's performance management system was gathered and the way in which managers used their performance management system was discussed. The management styles of regular and irregular performance management system users were also discussed in more detail with the interviewees. Exhibit 5.14 contains the interview protocol. The remainder of this section gives a summary of the answers most frequently given by the interviewees.

Summarizing, it can be said that the interviewees indicated they used the performance management system mainly for monitoring the performance and results of their organization; focusing their attention on spe-

Exhibit 5.13 **Correlation Matrix of Responsibility Areas with the Management Style Factors**

				Management Styles Factors		
Responsibility Area		*Conceptual Thinking*	*Flexibility & Adaptation*	*Teamwork & Cooperation*	*Communication*	*Analytical Thinking*
V1_7 (Number of employees the manager is directly responsible for)	Correlation	**.272**	-.027	.121	-.192	.023
	Significance	**.002**	.387	.104	**.022**	.405
V1_8 (Number of employees the manager is indirectly responsible for)	Correlation	.032	-.016	**.153**	.032	.081
	Significance	.378	.438	**.067**	.378	.215
V1_9 (Number of organizational units the manager is directly responsible for)	Correlation	**.176**	**.125**	-.042	.053	-.101
	Significance	**.032**	**.095**	.331	.290	.147
V1_10 (Number of organizational units the manager is indirectly responsible for)	Correlation	.083	.093	.061	.135	.015
	Significance	.222	.193	.286	.105	.444

Exhibit 5.14 **Interview Protocol**

Interview Part	*Purpose/Questions*
Explain goal of the interview	■ To obtain information on use of the PM systems (reports) ■ To obtain information on opinion of interviewee about characteristics of good performance management system users
Content of the interview	*Further acquaintance:* ■ Clarify research goals ■ Explain what will be done with the results ■ Explain why the research and its results are useful to the organization *Questions concerning the management report(s):* ■ Which management report(s) do you use? ■ Does this report contain mainly financial or nonfinancial information? Or both? ■ Who uses the report apart from yourself? ■ Is the report being used dynamically? In other words, are the performance indicators regularly revised? And, if so, by whom? ■ How is the IT support for the reports? ■ How frequently is the report produced? ■ What can you tell about the report layout? ■ What are, in your opinion, the main effects of the report (e.g., more control, higher revenues)? *Questions concerning the use of the management report(s):* ■ In what ways do you generally use the management report(s)? Are you using it for management control, to justify or answer for your decisions, for communicating, for evaluating projects/employees? ■ Can you give examples? ■ Do you experience the use of the management report(s) as useful and/or sensible? Why? *Questions concerning users of the management report(s):* ■ What qualities should people have, in your opinion, in order to be able to make successful use of the management report(s); one could think of knowledge, skills, attitudes, management style? ■ Can you give an example?

cific, important issues; formulating and factually supporting decisions and action plans; communicating more effectively; and motivating themselves and others to strive for continuous improvement. According to the interviewees, regular users of a performance management system have the following management styles:

- *They have analytical and conceptual skills.* Managers with this management style are able to identify the key points and see the cause-and-effect relationships. They also have an integral view of the business process. They are able to process information quickly and effectively and to link leading with lagging indicators.
- *They have content knowledge.* Managers with this management style have clear insight into the objectives and goals of their organization and their business unit. They also have a clear overview of the processes, products/services, trends, results, and consequences of these results.
- *They have communication skills.* Managers with this management style are able to listen and are proficient at asking questions. They can also place themselves in someone else's position.
- *They are good managers/coaches.* Managers with this management style set an example to employees and fellow managers by using the performance management system often and visibly. They also motivate and support their employees in using the performance management system and continuously look for improvement opportunities.
- *They are able to delegate.* Managers with this management style give employees enough freedom of action and rely on the skills and insights of these people.
- *They are good "time managers" and set priorities well.* Managers with this management style are proactive and focused in the sense that they decide and act on their priorities on the basis of the information of the performance management system, instead of being incapacitated by information overload.
- *They have vision and guts.* Managers with this management style are not afraid to break with the old ways of working and are open for change and new solutions.

If the answers given during the interviews are compared with the results from the correlation matrices (Exhibits 5.5 and 5.7), it turns out that some correlations are supported and others are not. Most of the mentioned skills and management styles were analytical and conceptual, which, according to the interviewees, are essential to be able to use a performance management system regularly. However, the theory and correlation matrix of Exhibit 5.5 only partially supports this opinion. A possible explanation for this discrepancy is that any manager needs analytical and conceptual skills to do the job properly, and therefore, these management styles are not specific for a regular or irregular performance management system user. This explanation is supported by the findings in the correlation matrix of Exhibit 5.7, which shows that respondents indicated that the management styles *conceptual thinking* and *flexibility and adaptation* are important for obtaining performance goals.

Many of the other skills mentioned during the interviews can more or less be seen in the light of a communicative manager. Delegation and time management skills as well as vision and guts are all essential to function properly in the turbulent environment in which modern managers operate.

DISCUSSION OF RESULTS

Part two of the investigation started with drafting a causal flow model (see Exhibit 4.4), from which several assumptions were derived about the management styles that a manager should have to be(come) a regular applier of certain types of performance management system use. By grouping the assumptions that after testing could not be rejected, answers can be found for the questions of the second investigation: *Which management styles are related to which types of performance management system use?* and *Do specific management styles and types of performance management system use have an effect on organizational performance?*

First, managers who are proficient in communication use a performance management system especially for decision support. Managers who are proficient in analytical thinking use a performance management system mainly for communication. Second, this use of a performance management system (for decision support, work integration, and communication) influences organizational performance favorably, especially the level of innovation. Third, certain management styles (conceptual thinking, flexibility and adaptation, teamwork and cooperation, and communication) also influence organizational performance favorably. Finally, the frequency and specific use of a performance management system does not depend on the age or experience of a manager.

In conclusion, it can be stated that the assumption made after the analysis of part one of the investigation—namely, that the factor of management styles of the controlled system (a manager) can play an important role in the successful implementation and regular use of a performance management system—proved to be a well-founded one. Linking the results of part one (see Exhibit 3.19) with those of part two gives the following overview of the areas to which organizations have to pay special attention during implementation of a new performance management system, in order to increase the chance of implementing a performance management system that will be regularly used (Exhibit 5.15):

Exhibit 5.15 **Overview of the Behavioral Factors and Management Styles, Important to the Implementation of a Regularly Used Performance Management System**

Classification Scheme Part	Areas of Attention to Obtain a Regularly Used Performance Management System	Behavioral Factors and Management Styles
Performance management system	Managers' understanding— *A good understanding by managers of the nature of performance management*	■ D4. Managers understand the meaning of KPIs. ■ D7. Managers have insight into the relationship between business processes and CSFs/KPIs. ■ U7. Managers' frames of reference contain similar KPIs. ■ U21. Managers agree on changes in the CSF/KPI set.
	Managers' management styles— *Management styles and related behaviors managers need to have to be(come) regular users of a performance management system*	■ CO. Proficiency at communication, for using a performance. ■ AT. Proficiency at analytical thinking, for using a performance management system for communication purposes.
Controlled system	Managers' attitude— *A positive attitude of managers toward performance management, performance management system, and the project*	■ S2. Managers agree on the starting time. ■ S4. Managers have earlier (positive) experiences with performance management. ■ U13. Managers realize the importance of CSFs/KPIs/BSC to their performance. ■ U14. Managers do not experience CSFs/KPIs/BSC as threatening.
Controlling system	Performance management system alignment— *A good match between managers' responsibilities and the performance management system*	■ D9. Manager's KPI sets are aligned with their responsibility areas. ■ D13. Managers can influence the KPIs assigned to them. ■ U9. Managers are involved in making analyses. ■ U15. Managers can use their CSFs/KPIs/BSC for managing their employees.

Exhibit 5.15   **Continued**

Classification Scheme Part	*Areas of Attention to Obtain a Regularly Used Performance Management System*	*Behavioral Factors and Management Styles*
Internal environment	Organizational culture—*An organizational culture focused on using the performance management system to improve*	■ U13. Managers' results on CSFs/KPIs/BSC are openly communicated. ■ U27. Managers are stimulated to improve their performance. ■ U8. Managers trust the performance information. ■ U17. Managers clearly see the promoter using the performance management system.
	Managers' management styles—*Management styles and related behaviors managers need to have to support organizational performance*	■ CO. Proficiency at communication, to obtain productivity and quality goals. ■ CT. Proficiency at conceptual thinking, to obtain productivity and quality goals. ■ FA. Proficiency at flexibility and adaptation, to obtain quality goals. ■ TC. Proficiency at teamwork and cooperation, to obtain productivity goals.
External environment	Performance management system focus—*A clear focus of the performance management system on internal management and control*	■ D16. Managers find the performance management system relevant because it has a clear, internal control purpose. ■ D17. Managers find the performance management system relevant because only those stakeholders interests are incorporated that are important to the organization's success.

The results of part one (see Exhibit 3.20) and part two can also be combined to group the least important behavioral factors and management styles together into categories, in such a way that an overview appears of the areas an organization does not have to pay special attention to when implementing a new performance management system (Exhibit 5.16).

Exhibit 5.16 **Overview of the Behavioral Factors and Management Styles, Least Important to the Implementation of a Regularly Used Performance Management System**

Classification Scheme Part	*Areas of Least Attention to Obtain a Regularly Used Performance Management System*	*Behavioral Factors and Management Styles*
Performance management system	Managers' involvement—*Direct involvement of managers in developing the new performance management system*	■ S3. Managers have been involved in decision making around the project start time. ■ D1. Managers have an active role during the development stage of the performance management system project. ■ D2. Managers are informed about the status of the performance management system project. ■ D3. Managers are actively communicating about the performance management system project. ■ D5. Managers are involved in defining KPIs. ■ D8. Managers are involved in setting KPI targets. ■ D10. Managers are involved in making the CSF/KPI/BSC report layout. ■ D11. Managers understand the CSF/KPI/BSC reporting.
	Managers' management styles—*Management styles and related behaviors managers need to have to be(come) regular users of a performance management system*	■ CO. Managers do not seem to need proficiency for communication (when using a performance management system for work integration and communication purposes). ■ CT. Managers do not seem to need proficiency for conceptual thinking (when using a performance management system for decision support, work integration, or communication purposes). ■ AT. Managers do not seem to need proficiency for analytical thinking (when using a

Exhibit 5.16 **Continued**

Classification Scheme Part	Areas of Least Attention to Obtain a Regularly Used Performance Management System	Behavioral Factors and Management Styles
Performance management system *(continued)*	Managers' management styles *(continued)*	performance management system for decision support and work integration purposes). ■ FA. Managers do not seem to need proficiency for flexibility and adaptation (when using a performance management system for decision support, work integration, or communication purposes). ■ TC. Managers do not seem to need proficiency for teamwork and cooperation (when using a performance management system for decision support, work integration, or communication purposes).
Controlled system		–
Controlling system		■ D14. Managers accept the promoter. ■ U16. Managers have sole responsibility for a KPI.
Internal environment	Managers' management styles—*Management styles and related behaviors managers need to have to support organizational performance*	■ AT. Managers do not seem to need proficiency for analytical thinking (to obtain productivity and quality goals). ■ FA. Managers do not seem to need proficiency for flexibility and adaptation (to obtain productivity goals). ■ TC. Managers do not seem to need proficiency for teamwork and cooperation (to obtain productivity goals).
External environment		–

CONCLUSION

The aim of the investigation described in this book was to identify the behavioral factors important to successful implementation and regular use of a performance management system. Initially, the research concentrated on identifying behavioral factors that were predicted by the literature to be influential on successful performance management system use. As a result, 18 behavioral factors were identified to which organization have to pay adequate attention in order to heighten their chance on a successful, that is, regularly and frequently used, performance management system.

The results from the investigation showed that additional research into some personal characteristics of managers was required. This meant a second investigation was started, which focused on management styles. This second investigation yielded several relations between specific management styles and specific performance management system uses. In addition, this second investigation showed that managers who use a performance management system and who possess several specific management styles can expect a better performance. The good news in this respect is that the age and experience of the manager has no effect on the use of a performance management system, so there are no barriers there. The consequence of this second investigation is that it is well worth the while for organizations to implement a performance management system that will be used regularly. In order to promote this regular use, organizations should develop and nurture specific management styles in their managers.

If organizations pay attention to both the 18 behavioral factors and the specific management styles, they will be able to develop, implement, and use a more well-balanced performance management system. In this respect, the results of the investigation described in this book yielded the features of a performance management system and its users, which make it possible for organizations to implement more well-balanced systems that will be used more regularly and frequently by the managers of an organization than is the case with more traditional systems.

ENDNOTES

1. Kaplan, R. S., and D. P. Norton (2000). *The strategy-focused organization: How balanced scorecard companies thrive in the new business environment.* Boston: Harvard Business School Press.

2. Kröger, F., M. Träum, and M. Vandenbosch (1998). *Spearheading growth: How Europe's top companies are restructuring to win.* London: Pitman Publishing.

3. Hackett (2000). *2000 Hackett benchmark solutions book of numbers for planning and performance measurement.* Hudson, Ohio: Answer Think Consulting Group.

4. Frigo, M. (2000). "Current trends in performance measurement systems." In: A. Neely, ed., *Performance measurement—past, present and future.* Cranfield, United Kingdom: Centre for Business Performance, Cranfield University, 153–160.

5. Katz, D., and R. L. Kahn (1978). *The social psychology of organizations.* New York: John Wiley & Sons.

APPENDICES

Appendix A
CASE STUDY
PROTOCOL

This appendix contains the activity plan, interview list, document research question list, questionnaire, and feedback reporting list of topics that were used in the case study research described in Part One of this book.

ACTIVITY PLAN

The activity plan provides a brief description of the activities to be performed during the case study.

Steps	Activities
1. Prepare the case study	■ Collect and study documentation about the organization. ■ Conduct introduction interview with the contact persons. ■ Agree on research scope, research timing, and research deliverable. ■ Inform the organization about the upcoming study. ■ Select interviewees. ■ Make appointments for the interviews.
2. Execute the questionnaires	■ Draft the questionnaire. ■ Select participants. ■ Distribute the questionnaires among the selected performance management system users. ■ Process the questionnaires.
3. Execute the document research	■ Collect and study documentation about the performance management system project and the performance management system itself.

Steps	*Activities*
	■ Study performance management system IT system (if present) and performance management system reports. ■ Document findings. ■ Give feedback and discuss findings with contact persons.
4. Execute the interviews	■ Draft interview protocol. ■ Conduct interviews with (at least) two management team members, controller, three product managers, the information manager, and performance management system project manager. ■ Make interview write-ups. ■ Feed back write-ups to interviewees and obtain approval. ■ Finalize interview write-ups.
5. Analyze and give feedback	■ Analyze the findings from questionnaire, document research, and interviews. ■ Draft conclusions and recommendations. ■ Make case description. ■ Formally present analyses and results to the organization. ■ Finalize case description. ■ Obtain approval for case description.

INTERVIEW LIST

A. Starting Point

2   When did the company start with the development of the performance management system project? Was this, according to you, a right moment? If yes, why? If no, why not?

3   Were you involved in the decision making of the performance management system project? If yes, in what way? If no, why not?

4   Did you have earlier experiences with performance measurement? If yes, what kind? Was this a positive or negative experience? Which effect had this experience on your attitude toward the development of CSF/KPIs?

5   Do you think that the use of CSF/KPIs is important for the continuity of the organization? If yes, why? If no, why not?

33 How do you describe the environment in which you work in the organization (stable/turbulent)? Why?

B. Development of the Performance Management System

8   Do the current CSFs and KPIs measure the strategy of the company? If yes, what CSFs and KPIs? If no, why not?

9   Do you agree that the right KPIs are chosen for your responsibilities inside the company?

10   Does there, according to you, exist a clear relationship exist between the CSFs and KPIs and the (crucial) business activities of the company? If yes, which? If no, why not?

12   Were you satisfied with your degree of involvement in the performance management system development process? How much and what role did you play (active/passive)?

13   Were you involved in the development of the definitions of the KPIs? If yes, how?

14   Are you involved in the determination of the content and the layout of the performance management system and CSF/KPI reports?

15   Who are, according to you, the initiator and promoter of the performance management system project? How do you judge/criticize their role?

32   Do you accept the responsibility for the KPIs that are appointed to you?

34   How much time (in hours and as a percentage of his time) did the promoter spend on the project?

38   Do you know the ins and outs of the definitions? How are the definitions available? How often are they changed?

41   How often, during the performance management system project, were you kept informed about the progress of the project? Did you appreciate this communication? If yes, why? If no, why not?

42   Who are the external stakeholders? To which degree do they have an influence on the content of the CSF/KPI set? How often do conflicts take place about this set with them?

43   What, in your opinion, was the focus during the development of the CSFs and KPIs: external or internal?

44   How often did you yourself contribute to the communication?

45   During the communication, were you asked for feedback? Give examples.

46   Was something done with the feedback you gave? Give examples.

47   Do the developed CSFs and KPIs give you a clear (good) view of all of the important aspects of your operating (management) level?

48   What was, according to you, the point of view at the development of CSFs and KPIs, internal or external?

C. Use of the Performance Management System

6   Do you find the use of the performance management system important for your role as manager? If yes, why? If no, why not?

11   Does any cause-and-effect relationship exist between the KPIs? If yes, how much? If no, why not?

16   Did you make any suggestions for changes in the performance management system, CSFs, and KPIs? If yes, were these suggestions taken into account?

17   To whom do you report your CSF/KPI results? Does he or she also work with the performance management system, CSFs, KPIs, and BSC? Is this, according to you, adequately visible (for the others) in the company?

19   Do you recognize any relationship between the results of the KPIs and the actions and financial results of the company? If yes, are you able to quantify this relationship? If yes, how? If no, why not?

20   Were you satisfied with the degree of involvement in the development of forecasts/prognosis? If yes, how do you make these forecasts/prognosis?

21   Do you feel threatened by the results of the indicators? If yes, why? If no, why not?

22   Do conflicts about the results of the indicators take place in your company?

23   Are there KPIs for which more than one manager is responsible for the results? If yes, how are possible conflicts relating to the determination of responsibilities solved?

24   Does there exist, according to you, a familiar relationship (of mutual confidence) between you and your boss/managers/employees?

25   How do you control your employees/managers (strict/loose)? How are you controlled by your boss?

26   Do you see any advantages or disadvantages of performance measurement in the way the people in the company are directed? If yes, what are these (dis)advantages? If no, why not?

28   How open are you in making your analysis? How serious is the conversation about the analysis of the results?

29   Does someone talk to you about the results of the CSFs and KPIs concerning your responsibilities? Do you talk to your employees about their results?

30   How much time do you spend on working with the performance management system and KPIs every time? Do you find this time enough?

30a   Are you able to spend enough time (effort) working with the performance management system and KPIs, compared to your other activities in the company?

35   Does a connection exist between the results of the performance management system and KPIs and your personal rewards? Are you happy with this connection? If yes, why? If no, why not?

39   How do you characterize the culture in your company (a culture of improvement or of settlement)? Why? Give examples.

50   To what degree do you determine actions on the CSFs and KPIs results? If yes, can you give an example? If no, why not?

51   Are the actions you take now better (more effective) compared to earlier times?

53 To what extent do you use the CSFs and KPIs for comparison of your results with: (a) other units of the company and (b) other companies? What are the advantages? If not used for comparison, why not?

54 Do you frequently make an analysis of the results of the CSF and KPIs? If yes, how do you make this analysis?

55 For how long did you work together with your employees/boss? Does this have any positive or negative influence about the implementation of the performance management system? Why?

56 Do you experience the comparison of company results as a threat? If yes, why?

58 Do discussions about the reliability of the performance management system frequently take place in the organization?

59 In time, did the results of the forecasts compared to the real results improve?

D. Successful Use of the Performance Management System

---

18 Do you frequently use the performance management system? How do you use it?

27 Do the managers talk frequently to each other about the results of the CSFs and KPIs? If yes, how often? If no, why not?

31 Has your performance improved through the use of the performance management system?

36 In time, did you make more or less use of the performance management system and why?

37 Are there, according to you, any future plans for the continuation of the performance management system project? If yes, what plans are made? If no, why not?

40 Is there something you want to talk about that we haven't discussed so far?

DOCUMENT RESEARCH QUESTION LIST

B. Development of the Performance Management System

---

11 Can an unambiguous and clear link between the CSFs and KPIs and the business functions/activities be found in the performance management system and reporting set?

20 To what extent are colors used in the performance management system and reporting set?

21 To what extent are tables used in the performance management system and reporting set?

22 To what extent are graphs used in the performance management system and reporting set?

23   To what extent are targets used in the performance management system and reporting set?

24   To what extent are standards layouts used in the performance management system and reporting set?

25   What is the appearance of the performance management system and reporting set? Is it understandable and easily accessible?

27   Are responsible managers appointed for all CSFs and KPIs?

28   Is one manager responsible for each KPI?

36   Can an unambiguous and clear link between the CSFs and KPIs and the strategy be found in the performance management system and reporting set?

37   Is there a separate CSF/KPI set for each management level?

38   Is there a separate external reporting set, or is the internal reporting set also used for external reporting purposes?

C. Use of the Performance Management System

---

12   Are analyses and progress and results of actions incorporated in the performance management system?

19   How often (per month/year) are forecasts made?

29   Are financial consequences of actions mentioned in the performance management system?

30   What is the quality of the analyses, as seen in the performance management system?

31   Does mutual comparison of results take place between the managers (ranking)?

32   Are forecasts improved in comparison to the actuals?

34   Are evaluations of the performance management system available? If yes, evaluate the quality of these evaluations.

35   Are CSFs and KPIs part of the yearly planning cycle?

D. Successful Use of the Performance Management System

---

8   Have the results of the company improved as a consequence of using the performance management system? If yes, how much improvement (%) has been realized? If no, why not?

33   Review the plans (if available) for the next project phase.

39   What is the number of users of the performance management system?

40   What is the frequency of use (number of times per month)?

E. General Company Information

---

1   Branch

2   National/International

3   Independent/Part of a conglomerate

4	Organizational structure
5	Mission/Strategy of the company: content, focus (clients, costs, etc.), how long in place
6	Average age of management
7	Current situation: turnover, margin, number of employees, number of managers
10	Percentage financial vs. nonfinancial information
13	Number of CSFs and KPIs defined
14	Which kind of CSFs and KPIs are used (strategic, functional/tactical/operational)?
15	Frequency of reporting
16	Are specific definitions and targets used?
17	Are the definitions of the KPIs documented? If yes, how?
18	Volume of the periodic reporting set (in number of pages)
26	Name of the performance management system project

QUESTIONNAIRE

The questionnaire contains 19 questions that for the most part can be answered according to this scheme: 1 = completely disagree; 2 = partially disagree; 3 = partially agree; 4 = completely agree.

No.	Questions	Answers
1a.	Were there sufficient reasons for implementing a performance management system? Options: ■ Lack of operational data ■ Lack of insight into the execution of the strategy ■ Lack of insight into the results of crucial organizational processes ■ Reporting not action oriented enough ■ Lack of insight into developments in the market (competition, customer focus) ■ Other	1/2/3/4
1b.	What was, according to you, the main goal of implementing a performance management system? Options: ■ There was a relation with implementing the new strategy ■ For accountability purposes ■ For benchmarking purposes ■ Not clear	1/2/3/4

No.	Questions	Answers
2	I had a positive attitude toward the implementation of the performance management system, CSFs, KPIs, and BSC.	1/2/3/4
3	I was (actively) involved during definition making of the KPIs.	1/2/3/4
4	I was sufficiently involved during the final choosing of the KPIs.	1/2/3/4
5	What percentage of the total data needed in the performance management system is manually provided by you?	More than 75%/ between 25 and 75%/less than 25%
6	The time my subordinates and I spend on collecting data for KPI reporting is acceptable.	1/2/3/4
7	I was sufficiently involved during the setting of targets for the KPIs.	1/2/3/4
8	My suggestions and wishes for changes in the CSF/KPI set have been sufficiently implemented.	1/2/3/4
9	The current CSF/KPI set measures the strategic goals of the organization adequately.	1/2/3/4
10	There exists an unambiguous relationship between the CSF/KPI set and the crucial business activities of the organization.	1/2/3/4
11	The current CSF/KPI set is an adequate reflection of my responsibility area.	1/2/3/4
12	The manner in which the performance management system reports and shows CSFs, KPIs, and BSC is understandable and easily accessible.	1/2/3/4
13	The reported results are reliable.	1/2/3/4
14	I am sufficiently involved during the making of analyses.	1/2/3/4
15	How often do you discuss the KPI results with other people in the organization?	Once per month/ once per quarter/ less than once per month/other time frame
16	I currently have a positive attitude toward the use of the performance management system, CSFs , KPIs and BSC: YES/NO	1/2/3/4
17	The performance management system, CSFs, KPIs, and BSC play an import role during my activities.	1/2/3/4

No.	*Questions*	*Answers*
18	My results and those of my subordinates have improved as a consequence of using the performance management system.	1/2/3/4
19	Room for additional remarks:	

FEEDBACK REPORTING LIST OF TOPICS

This feedback reporting list of topics contains a list of topics that have to be addressed in the case description.

Topic	*Content*
1. Description of the company	<ul><li>Branch</li><li>Products and services</li><li>Mission and strategy</li><li>Turnover and number of personnel</li><li>Organizational structure</li></ul>
2. History of the performance management system project	<ul><li>The reason for starting the project</li><li>Situation of the company at the starting time</li><li>Time span of the project</li><li>Project approach (including description of the project team)</li><li>Description (brief, concise) of the three project stages: starting, development, use</li><li>Current situation of the company</li><li>Current status of the project</li></ul>
3. Content performance management system	<ul><li>Examples of the CSFs and KPIs</li><li>Examples of the BSC and other management reporting formats</li><li>Examples of the IT solution (if present)</li><li>Number of CSFs, KPIs, BSC, and other management reports</li><li>Description of the target audiences for the CSFs, KPIs, and BSC</li></ul>

Topic	*Content*
4. Case study research	■ Reasons for researching this company ■ Description (brief, concise) of the research steps ■ Description of the results of the questionnaire ■ Description of the results of the interviews ■ Description of the results of the document analysis
5. Results of the case study research	■ Summary of the results ■ Detailed description of the results, per project stage ■ Detailed description of the results on the criteria for regular use

Appendix B
QUESTIONNAIRE

This appendix contains the questionnaire that was distributed to the 11 organizations described in Part Two of this book.

QUESTIONNAIRE PERFORMANCE EVALUATION:
HOW MANAGERS USE INFORMATION

1.   Personal Data

1.1   Age

_____ years

1.2   Gender

❏ Male

❏ Female

1.3   How many years of experience do you have in your current profession?

_____ years

1.4   How many years of experience do you have in your current function?

_____ years

1.5   How many hours a week do you work?

      _____ hours

1.6   How many hours a week do you spend on management tasks? *(It is quite possible that the answer to this question is equal to your answer to the previous question. If you do not only have managerial responsibility, but also take part in the primary processes of your organization, the number of hours will differ.)*

      _____ hours

1.7   How many employees are you *directly* responsible for? *(If you are responsible for four persons, who in turn are responsible for ten persons each, you are directly responsible for four persons and indirectly for forty.)*

      _____ employees

1.8   How many employees are you *indirectly* responsible for?

      _____ employees

1.9   How many organizational units are under your *direct* responsibility?

      _____ organizational units

1.10 How many organizational units are under your *indirect* responsibility?

      _____ organizational units

2.   Use of the Management Information

2.1   How many hours do you spend on analyzing/studying the reports (excluding appendices) each time you receive one?

      _____ hours

2.2   How many hours do you spend on analyzing/studying the appendices to the reports each time you receive the report?

      _____ hours

      ❑ There are no appendices

2.3   Apart from the periodic reports, special investigations may take place in order to obtain more insight into the performance of your organizational unit. What is the importance of those investigations?

They are not carried out at all	They are relatively unimportant	They are less important than the periodic reports	They are about as important as the periodic reports	They are more important than the periodic reports
❏	❏	❏	❏	❏

2.4 Some organizations provide managers the possibility to examine detailed transaction data of their own organizational unit by means of a special computer program. Do your have this possibility?

❏ No

❏ Yes, but I hardly use this possibility

❏ Yes, and I use it regularly

2.5 In order to exercise your function as a manager, do you mainly use financial or nonfinancial data?

Almost only nonfinancial information	Both, but non- financial data are most important	The importance of both kinds of information is about equal	Both, but financial data are most important	Almost only financial information
❏	❏	❏	❏	❏

2.6 In order to exercise your function as a manager, do you mainly use quantitative or qualitative information?

Almost only quantitative information	Both, but quantitative data are most important	The importance of both kinds of information is about equal	Both, but qualitative data are most important	Almost only qualitative information
❏	❏	❏	❏	❏

3. Appropriateness of Information

3.1 Are financial or nonfinancial measures, in your opinion, most appropriate to present the performance of your organizational unit?

Only nonfinancial measures are appropriate	Both, but nonfinancial measures are more appropriate	Both are about as appropriate	Both, but financial measures are more appropriate	Only financial measures are appropriate
❑	❑	❑	❑	❑

3.2 Are quantitative or qualitative measures in your opinion most appropriate to present the performance of your organizational unit?

Only qualitative measures are appropriate	Both, but qualitative measures are more appropriate	Both are about as appropriate	Both, but quantitative measures are more appropriate	Only quantitative measures are appropriate
❑	❑	❑	❑	❑

3.3 How appropriate are, in your opinion, traditional measures like profits, ROI (return on investment) and traditional cost figures, for managing your organizational unit in comparison with new measures like activity-based costing, shareholders value analysis, and EVA (economic value added)?

Traditional measures are sufficient	Traditional measures are reasonably sufficient	New measures complement traditional measures	New measures are as important as traditional measures	New measures are more important than traditional measures
❑	❑	❑	❑	❑

3.4 In order to exercise your function, is it necessary to monitor what is happening in the organization yourself (in other words your own observation of business processes), or do the regular management reports suffice?

For me, reports are almost useless; I completely depend on my own observation	My own observations are most important, but the reports are of importance as well	My own observations and the reports are about as important	The reports are most important, but my own observations are important as well	I completely depend on the reports; my own observation plays an inferior part
❏	❏	❏	❏	❏

4. Other Sources of Information

Apart from the official management information, you might use information from other sources to exercise your function as a manager. In the table underneath, a number of potential sources of information are mentioned. For each of these sources, indicate how important they are for exercising your function as a manager at the moment? *(Please check one alternative per source. If you do not use a source at all, check the alternative "very unimportant.")*

		Very important	Important	Some-what important	Unim-portant	Very unim-portant
4.1	Information from customers	❏	❏	❏	❏	❏
4.2	Information from competitors	❏	❏	❏	❏	❏
4.3	Information from suppliers	❏	❏	❏	❏	❏
4.4	Information from your own social network	❏	❏	❏	❏	❏
4.5	Information from television and radio	❏	❏	❏	❏	❏

	Very important	Important	Some-what important	Unimportant	Very unimportant
4.6 Information from newspapers	❏	❏	❏	❏	❏
4.7 Information from Internet	❏	❏	❏	❏	❏
4.8 Information from your industry organization	❏	❏	❏	❏	❏
4.9 Information obtained on congresses and seminars	❏	❏	❏	❏	❏
4.10 Information from professional journals	❏	❏	❏	❏	❏

4.11 How important are the sources mentioned above compared with the official management reports provided by your organization for the adequate assessment of the performance of your organization or organizational unit?

Much more important than the "official" reports	More important than the "official" reports	As important as the "official" reports	Less important than the "official" reports	Far less important than the "official" reports
❏	❏	❏	❏	❏

5. Your Organizational Unit

5.1 How many written rules and procedures exist for the tasks in your organizational unit?

Very few if any	A small number	A moderate number	A large number	A great number
❑	❑	❑	❑	❑

5.2 How precisely do these rules and procedures specify how the tasks in your organizational unit are to be done?

Very general	Mostly general	Somewhat specific	Quite specific	Very specific
❑	❑	❑	❑	❑

5.3 How strictly are these rules and procedures enforced in your organizational unit?

Not at all enforced	Very loosely enforced	Quite strictly enforced	Strictly enforced	Very strictly enforced
❑	❑	❑	❑	❑

5.4 How likely are you to notice it when those rules are broken?

Very small	Small	Not particularly large	Large	Very large
❑	❑	❑	❑	❑

6. Your Employees

6.1 With which frequency do you evaluate the employees that fall under your responsibility? *(If the exact amount is not mentioned, please choose the most similar frequency. Once every four weeks becomes once a month in that case.)*

Never	At most once a year	Once every half year	Once every three months	Once a month or more often
❑	❑	❑	❑	❑

6.2   Does your organizational unit use assessment centers and/or psychological tests?

❑ Yes, for all functions

❑ Yes, for a part of our personnel

❑ No

6.3   Approximately what proportion of your employees are members of a professional organization?

Hardly anyone	Less than 50%	About 50%	More than 50%	Almost everyone
❑	❑	❑	❑	❑

6.4   How often do your employees on average take part in courses or other forms of (continuing) education?

Hardly ever	Less than once every four years	At least once in four years	Once a year	More often than once a year
❑	❑	❑	❑	❑

6.5   Is the management in your organization originating from the own organization (could one speak of "own breed"), or are mostly persons from outside the own organization appointed to management positions?

Mostly originating from own organization	About 75% is "own breed"	About 50% is "own breed"	About 75% is from outside the own organization	Mostly external
❑	❑	❑	❑	❑

6.6 To what extent are you experienced in exercising the functions of your employees? *(If you are still working in the primary business process of your organizational unit, please check the first answer.)*

I have experience in my own organizational unit	I have experience elsewhere in my own organization	I have experience in another organization	I have theoretical, but no practical experience	I have no experience in these functions at all
❏	❏	❏	❏	❏

6.7 What is more important for the evaluation of the performance of your employees, their efforts or the results obtained?

Only efforts count	Efforts are more important than results	Both are equally important	Results are more important than efforts	Only results count
❏	❏	❏	❏	❏

6.8 If in your organizational unit a situation occurs in which a manager does not meet his or her budget, and the person involved is able to make clear that not meeting the budget is a consequence of decisions that will in the long run be better for the organization's performance as a whole than decisions made to meet the budget would have been, how would this manager be evaluated?

Negatively, the budget has not been met	Negatively, but less severe than without the motivation provided	Neutrally, the motivation provided compensates for not meeting the budget	Positively, but not meeting the budget also counts	Positively, the results of the organization as a whole will improve in the long run
❏	❏	❏	❏	❏

6.9   Do you take personal circumstances into account when evaluating your employees? *(With personal circumstances, we indicate circumstances in the personal lives of employees. Items like an educational trajectory or change of function are not considered to be personal circumstances.)*

Always	Most times	In about the half of cases	Seldom	Never
❏	❏	❏	❏	❏

6.10   Does your final evaluation have financial consequences for the employee involved? *(The term* financial consequences *is used to indicate situations in which the outcome of the evaluation is directly used to determine matters like change in salary or awarding [or denying] a bonus.)*

No, the evaluation does not have financial consequences	The evaluation has very small financial consequences	The evaluation has some financial consequences	The evaluation has financial consequences that are clearly perceivable	The evaluation has large financial consequences
❏	❏	❏	❏	❏

6.11   How important is your personal presence as a supervisor, advisor, informer, and the like for the quality of the performance of your employees?

If I am not present, performance quality is bad	If I am not present, performance quality suffers considerably	If I am not present, performance quality suffers	If I am not there, performance quality suffers slightly	My personal presence has little or no influence on performance quality
❏	❏	❏	❏	❏

6.12   Do official rules exist in your organization concerning the number of employees that have to be evaluated positively, negatively, or neutrally?

❑ Yes, those rules exist

❑ There are no official rules, but in practice there are target percentages

❑ No, those rules do not exist at all

6.13 How do you think your employees feel about the extent to which you meddle in the way they execute their tasks? *(Note: This question is aiming at determining the opinion of your employees; this opinion is not necessarily correct.)*

They would prefer to see me more involved	A little more involvement would be appreciated	They are content with the situation as it is	A little less involvement would be appreciated	They would prefer to see me less involved
❑	❑	❑	❑	❑

6.14 To what extent are you informed earlier than your employees about matters going on in your organizational unit?

In this organizational unit, I am the first to know everything	It happens only occasionally that someone else knows something earlier than I do	On details others may be informed earlier, but I am the first to know essential matters	On essential matters, I am usually informed first; on matters of details, only occasionally	Generally, my employees are informed earlier than I am
❑	❑	❑	❑	❑

7. Comparison of Results

How important is each of the following points of reference for evaluating the performance of your organization or organizational unit?

	Very important	Important	Some-what important	Unim-portant	Very unim-portant
7.1 Comparison with the budget	❑	❑	❑	❑	❑

	Very impor- tant	Impor- tant	Some- what impor- tant	Unim- portant	Very unim- portant
7.2 Comparison with the maximal attainable result	❑	❑	❑	❑	❑
7.3 Comparison with results in the last period	❑	❑	❑	❑	❑
7.4 Comparison with the results of other organizational units within the own organization	❑	❑	❑	❑	❑
7.5 Comparison with results of other organizational units of competing organizations (benchmarking)	❑	❑	❑	❑	❑

7.6 How often are targets revised during a budget period?

Hardly ever	Seldom	Regularly	Very regularly	Almost always
❑	❑	❑	❑	❑

8. Propositions about Your Organizational Unit

If you look at the way you manage your organizational unit, to what extent do you agree with the following propositions:

		Strongly agree	Agree	Neutral	Dis-agree	Strongly disagree
8.1	Simple performance measures suffice because I know what is going on in my organizational unit.	❏	❏	❏	❏	❏
8.2	I examine only the bottom line of financial results.	❏	❏	❏	❏	❏
8.3	If you already are going to miss your target, you better do it to a large extent, in order to make results in later periods look better.	❏	❏	❏	❏	❏
8.4	By hiring the right personnel, evaluation of performance is relatively unimportant.	❏	❏	❏	❏	❏
8.5	By taking care of a good culture in my organizational unit, I can depend on people doing their job as best as they are able to, which makes performance measurement essentially superfluous.	❏	❏	❏	❏	❏
8.6	You notice whether customers are satisfied only by monitoring the primary process.	❏	❏	❏	❏	❏

	Strongly agree	Agree	Neutral	Dis-agree	Strongly disagree
8.7 In financial reports, the items above the bottom line are mainly indicative of developments or trends.	❑	❑	❑	❑	❑
8.8 I do not have to look at the numbers accurately, as I regularly carry out a more elaborate evaluation.	❑	❑	❑	❑	❑
8.9 I manage by exception—as long as performance is satisfactory, people can do things their own way.	❑	❑	❑	❑	❑
8.10 The financial reports I receive contain the same information as is used for external reporting purposes (the annual report).	❑	❑	❑	❑	❑
8.11 The way I evaluate my employees is similar to the way my supervisors evaluate me.	❑	❑	❑	❑	❑

❑ Not applicable

	Strongly agree	Agree	Neutral	Dis-agree	Strongly disagree
8.12 The most recent management report is always within hands' reach.	❑	❑	❑	❑	❑

	Strongly agree	Agree	Neutral	Dis-agree	Strongly disagree
8.13 If it were not obligatory, I would not make formal evaluations of my subordinates.	❏	❏	❏	❏	❏

❏ Not applicable

	Strongly agree	Agree	Neutral	Dis-agree	Strongly disagree
8.14 If the results of the performance measurement system do not match your expectations, you should adjust the performance measurement system.	❏	❏	❏	❏	❏
8.15 The final evaluation of an employee is a formality. At the moment the evaluation report is finished, the employee already knows whether he or she will be evaluated positively or negatively.	❏	❏	❏	❏	❏
8.16 I occasionally have found myself in a situation in which I had to neglect long-term opportunities as I had to reach my targets for the current period first.	❏	❏	❏	❏	❏

9. Performance of the Organizational Unit

In relation to other comparable organizations or organizational units, how did your unit, in your opinion, rate on each of the following factors during the past year?

		Far below average	Some-what below average	About average	Some-what above average	Far above average
9.1	The quantity or amount of work produced	❑	❑	❑	❑	❑
9.2	The quality or accuracy of work produced	❑	❑	❑	❑	❑
9.3	The number of innovations or new ideas introduced	❑	❑	❑	❑	❑
9.4	Reputation for work excellence	❑	❑	❑	❑	❑
9.5	Attainment of unit productions or service goals	❑	❑	❑	❑	❑
9.6	Efficiency of unit operations	❑	❑	❑	❑	❑
9.7	Morale of personnel	❑	❑	❑	❑	❑
9.8	Development of revenues (if applicable)	❑	❑	❑	❑	❑

❑ Not applicable

	Far below average	Some- what below average	About average	Some- what above average	Far above average
9.9 Development of profits (if applicable)	❏	❏	❏	❏	❏

❏ Not applicable

10. Use of the System

The following questions are not about the management reports as a whole, but only about the balanced scorecard (BSC).

	Strongly agree	Agree	Neutral	Dis- agree	Strongly disagree
10.1 I use the BSC to help me make explicit the reasons for my decisions.	❏	❏	❏	❏	❏
10.2 I use the BSC to improve the effectiveness and efficiency of the decision process.	❏	❏	❏	❏	❏
10.3 I use the BSC to check my thinking against the data.	❏	❏	❏	❏	❏
10.4 My organizational unit and I use the BSC to coordinate our activities.	❏	❏	❏	❏	❏
10.5 I use the BSC to coordinate activities with others in my organizational unit.	❏	❏	❏	❏	❏

		Strongly agree	Agree	Neutral	Dis-agree	Strongly disagree
10.6	I use the BSC to communicate with people who report to me.	❏	❏	❏	❏	❏
10.7	I use the BSC to communicate with people I report to.	❏	❏	❏	❏	❏
10.8	I use the BSC to make the decision process more rational.	❏	❏	❏	❏	❏
10.9	I use the BSC to deal more strategically with internal and/or external customers.	❏	❏	❏	❏	❏
10.10	I use the BSC to serve customers more creatively.	❏	❏	❏	❏	❏
10.11	I use the BSC to monitor my own performance.	❏	❏	❏	❏	❏
10.12	I use the BSC to plan my work.	❏	❏	❏	❏	❏
10.13	I use the BSC to serve internal and/or external customers.	❏	❏	❏	❏	❏
10.14	I use the BSC to decide how to best approach a problem.	❏	❏	❏	❏	❏
10.15	I use the BSC to get feedback on job performance.	❏	❏	❏	❏	❏

	Strongly agree	Agree	Neutral	Dis-agree	Strongly disagree
10.16 I use the BSC to help me justify my decisions.	❏	❏	❏	❏	❏
10.17 I use the BSC to improve the quality of customer service.	❏	❏	❏	❏	❏
10.18 I use the BSC to communicate with other people in my organizational unit.	❏	❏	❏	❏	❏
10.19 I use the BSC to analyze why problems occur.	❏	❏	❏	❏	❏
10.20 I use the BSC to help me explain my decisions.	❏	❏	❏	❏	❏
10.21 I use the BSC to make sense out of data.	❏	❏	❏	❏	❏
10.22 I use the BSC to exchange information with internal and/or external customers.	❏	❏	❏	❏	❏

11. Propositions

Hereinafter, 35 propositions concerning behaviors are listed. Indicate for each of them whether you show that behavior never, sometimes, often, or always.

	Never	Sometimes	Often	Always
11.1 I take rational decisions, even if my feelings tell me to take alternative ones.	❏	❏	❏	❏

		Never	Sometimes	Often	Always
11.2	With many problems, I am not interested in what the causes were; they just have to be solved immediately!	❏	❏	❏	❏
11.3	I encourage others to visit me for support, advice, or encouragement.	❏	❏	❏	❏
11.4	I hang on to successful approaches as long as possible, even when I know the circumstances are changing.	❏	❏	❏	❏
11.5	When trying to understand a problem, I work it out to identify its different aspects.	❏	❏	❏	❏
11.6	When I need to judge a situation, I look at the available information.	❏	❏	❏	❏
11.7	I share the credit with everyone who contributed to a success, even if I was the main coordinator responsible.	❏	❏	❏	❏
11.8	I avoid listening to other persons' point of view when I have already formed my own opinion.	❏	❏	❏	❏
11.9	After I have given a presentation, people ask me to give further clarifications.	❏	❏	❏	❏

	Never	Sometimes	Often	Always

11.10 When I want to solve a complex problem, I try to redefine it into concepts that are recognizable to me. ❏ ❏ ❏ ❏

11.11 When performing a task that is new to me, I first investigate how it is related to other tasks that I performed before. ❏ ❏ ❏ ❏

11.12 When someone is speaking to me (or to an audience that I am in), I am able to stop thinking instantly about anything else and concentrate on what is being said. ❏ ❏ ❏ ❏

11.13 When facing a problem, I immediately take a decision, without first considering a number of possible alternatives. ❏ ❏ ❏ ❏

11.14 I can get so intensively focused on specific details that I forget the big picture. ❏ ❏ ❏ ❏

11.15 I repeat something that someone says to me in my own words to ensure that I have understood the message correctly. ❏ ❏ ❏ ❏

11.16 I have a variety of writing styles from which I choose the most appropriate for the reader to whom I am addressing my correspondence. ❏ ❏ ❏ ❏

	Never	Sometimes	Often	Always
11.17 I express my opinion or expectations only when I expect people to accept them.	❑	❑	❑	❑
11.18 I encourage others in a group to work together.	❑	❑	❑	❑
11.19 I combine relevant information and concepts from several very different sources to get a clear picture of the situation.	❑	❑	❑	❑
11.20 My "intuition" and feelings guide the decisions that I finally make.	❑	❑	❑	❑
11.21 I consciously consider several different approaches before tackling a problem.	❑	❑	❑	❑
11.22 I am quite selective when it comes to sharing my information or knowledge with others.	❑	❑	❑	❑
11.23 At business meetings, I pursue meeting people who are newly present.	❑	❑	❑	❑
11.24 On issues that relate to my work, I decide on my own, even if I am part of a group.	❑	❑	❑	❑
11.25 I am uncomfortable when I have to handle several things at once.	❑	❑	❑	❑
11.26 I adapt quickly to changes in my work situation.	❑	❑	❑	❑

	Never	Sometimes	Often	Always
11.27 When I hear that someone else in my team needs resources that I possess, I immediately offer to share some of these resources with him or her.	❏	❏	❏	❏
11.28 When confronted with an unexpected outcome, I make a list of sequential events that might have caused it.	❏	❏	❏	❏
11.29 I look at issues from different interest group perspectives.	❏	❏	❏	❏
11.30 I understand new things by seeing how they fit with what I already know.	❏	❏	❏	❏
11.31 I modify my approaches in accordance to changing circumstances.	❏	❏	❏	❏
11.32 I try to predict the potential consequences and future courses of events resulting from implementation of alternative courses of action.	❏	❏	❏	❏
11.33 I pay particular attention to others' feelings when expressing myself.	❏	❏	❏	❏
11.34 I don't pay attention to the layout of my reports: It is the content that counts.	❏	❏	❏	❏

	Never	Sometimes	Often	Always
11.35 I reassign members of a group to different tasks/ responsibilities to see what they are good at.	❑	❑	❑	❑

12. Questions and Comments

12.1   If you have any questions or comments, please use the space below.

Thank you for your cooperation!

INDEX